James W. (James William) Buel

The Border Bandits

An authentic and thrilling History of the noted Outlaws, Jesse and Frank James

James W. (James William) Buel

The Border Bandits
An authentic and thrilling History of the noted Outlaws, Jesse and Frank James

ISBN/EAN: 9783337159191

Printed in Europe, USA, Canada, Australia, Japan

Cover: Foto ©ninafisch / pixelio.de

More available books at **www.hansebooks.com**

THE BORDER BANDITS.

AN AUTHENTIC AND THRILLING HISTORY OF THE NOTED OUTLAWS,

JESSE & FRANK JAMES,

And their Bands of Highwaymen.

COMPILED FROM RELIABLE SOURCES ONLY AND CONTAINING THE LATEST FACTS IN REGARD TO THESE DESPERATE FREEBOOTERS.

BY J. W. BUEL,

Author of "Life of Wild Bill the Scout," "Legends of the Ozarks," etc., etc., and Member of the Editorial Staff of the Kansas City and St. Louis Press.

ILLUSTRATED WITH LATE PORTRAITS AND COLORED PLATES.

ST. LOUIS, MO.:
HISTORICAL PUBLISHING COMPANY.
1881.

PREFACE.

THE career of Jesse and Frank James has been as checkered as the sunlight that streams through a latticed window, and their crimes are a commentary upon the development of intellectual America. No one can afford to ignore the lesson which the lives of these outlaws teach, and therefore a correct history of their desperate deeds becomes necessary as a part of the country's annals, in juxtaposition with the commendable heroism of our brightest characters. So many improbable and romantic incidents have been credited to these noted brothers by sensational writers; so many dashing escapades and hair-breadth escapes attributed to them, which they never even dreamed of, that thinking people, especially in the East, have begun, almost, to regard the James Boys as a myth, and their deeds as creations of sensational dreamers.

It has been my purpose for more than three years to prepare a true history of these noted outlaws, and during that time material has been collecting which is now given to the public entirely free from fulsome description or elaborated sensation. In the main essentials the James Boys themselves will confirm the truthfulness of this narrative, which has been written with a special regard for candor and indisputable facts only.

During several years of the most exciting period in the career of these noted bandits, I was engaged as reporter for the Kansas City press, and not only became acquainted with many of their relatives and friends who reside in that section, from whom were obtained numerous facts and incidents never before published; but my duties as a journalist gave me many excellent opportunities to learn the real truth in regard to many of their most daring adventures, to one of which (the robbing of the cash-box at the Kansas City Fair) I was an eye-witness. As time unfolds the mysteries which have gathered around the names of these desperate outlaws, it will be seen that this is the most faithful history of their exploits that has ever been presented to the public. J. W. B.

St. Louis, December 15, 1880.

ILLUSTRATIONS.

	PAGE.
PORTRAITS OF THE JAMES BROTHERS. Frontispiece.	
After Centralia,	8
HANGING OF DR. SAMUELS,	10
Fleeing from Lawrence,	18
JESSE JAMES' RECEPTION,	38
Romantic Scenery near the Mysterious Cave,	44
Frank James' Combat with three Mexicans,	50
Recruiting after a Raid,	57
Hobbs Kerry watched by a Detective in a Gambling Den,	91
SHOOTING OF JESSE JAMES,	107
SETTLING AN OLD SCORE,	112
Frank James wins his Bride,	121
An Engineer who meant fight.	125

3 B.

AFTER CENTRALIA.—see p. 27.

THE BORDER BANDITS.

CONTENTS:

	PAGE.
JESSE AND FRANK JAMES—THEIR YOUTH,	7
Career as Guerrillas,	9
First Skirmishes,	12
Desolation of Lawrence,	15
Desperate Fighting by Squads,	21
Direful Massacre at Centralia,	27
Fortune Turning Against the Guerrillas,	30
The Whirlwind of Destruction Changes,	31
Jesse James' Career in Texas,	33
Robbery and Murder,	36
Plundering a Kentucky Bank,	39
Bank Robbery and Murder,	41
Mysterious Hiding Place in Jackson Co.,	43
Terrible Fight in Mexico,	47
Plundering an Iowa Bank,	51
Another Bank Robbery in Kentucky,	52
Robbing the Cash Box at the Kansas City Fair,	54
Plundering the Ste. Genevieve Bank,	56
Wrecking and Plundering a Train,	60
The Stage Robbery near Hot Springs,	63
Train Robbery at Gad's Hill,	66
Wicher's Unfortunate Hunt for the James Boys,	69
Murdering Cow Boys and Driving off Cattle,	73
The Attack on the Samuels' Residence,	75
Assassination of Daniel Askew,	79
The San Antonio Stage Robbery,	81

CONTENTS.

The Great Train Robbery at Muncie,	83
The Huntington Bank Robbery,	86
The Rocky Cut Train Robbery,	87
Fatal Attack on a Minnesota Bank,	92
At Glendale—the Last Great Train Robbery,	96
Shooting of Jesse James by George Shepherd,	100
Why did Shepherd Shoot Jesse James?	109
Robbing of the Mammoth Cave Stage,	112
Personal Characteristics of the James Boys,	117
The Union Pacific Express Robbery,	122
An Interview with the Younger Brothers,	132
Anecdotes of Jesse and Frank James,	138

THE BORDER BANDITS.

JESSE AND FRANK JAMES.

THEIR YOUTH.

STRANGELY, and yet a not uncommon circumstance, Jesse and Frank James were the sons of a respectable Kentucky minister of the Baptist persuasion. Rev. Robt. James, "in the good old times," as he was wont to call the early days of his ministry, was a great camp-meeting exhorter, and many of the rock-ribbed hills of middle Kentucky have been musical with the echoes of his strong voice. Like many other pastoral exhorters and close communionists, the Rev. James was illiterate so far as "book learning" was concerned, but his sincerity was rarely debated. It has been asserted that he passed an academic course at Georgetown College, but the records of that institution show the name of no such person. Zerelda Cole, (the mother of the noted outlaws,) was married to the Rev. Robert James in Scott county, Kentucky, the same county in which Georgetown College is located; this fact, added to the desire to heroize, to the largest possible extent, the paternity of the James boys, is doubtless the reason for ascribing to the father "a finished education and unusual ability."

"Like father, like son," is a very ancient oriental adage; but it does not apply to Jesse and Frank James, though it is true that their dispositions are due to maternal inheritance. In fact, the wife's strength of will and uncompanionable traits of character resulted in a final separation a few years after their removal to Clay county, Missouri, in 1843. The Rev. James, in 1849, joined in the pilgrimage to California, from whence he never returned; and, in 1857, Mrs. James took another husband, in the person of Dr. Reuben Samuels. It is quite unimportant to follow the domestic career of Mrs. James, now Mrs. Samuels, and what has been related is merely for the purpose of defining the inherited bent and inclination of the parents of the great outlaws.

Jesse James was born in Clay county, Missouri, in 1845, while Frank's nativity is Scott county, Kentucky, where he was born in 1841. At an extremely early age they displayed traits of character which have ever since distinguished them. Their hatreds were always bitter and their cruelty remorseless. They manifested especial delight in punishing dumb animals, which is evidenced by their cutting off the tails and ears of dogs and cats, burying small animals alive, and diversions of every kind which would inflict the most grievous pains. Among other boys they were domineering and cruel, and would rarely participate in innocent amusements. They were never subjected to parental restraint and their youth was passed in the most perfect indulgence. At the age of ten and fourteen years, respectively, the boys were provided with fire-arms, in the use of which they readily became proficient, and were no less expert in throwing a bowie-knife which they could send quivering into a two-inch sapling, at the space of fifteen feet, almost without fail.

THEIR CAREER AS GUERRILLAS.

WHEN the tocsin of war sounded, and the feverish thrill of excitement ran through the nation, boys though they were, Jesse and Frank James were electrified with the ominous news and longed to participate in the affray where human blood might be drawn until, like a fountain, it would swell into a gory river. Soon the unmerciful Quantrell, that terrible wraith of slaughter, came trooping through Missouri upon an errand of destruction, and attracted to his banner many impetuous youths of the West, among whom was Frank James; Jesse being the junior brother, and but little more than fourteen years of age, was rejected by Quantrell, and returned home to his farm labors with sorrow. But he did not remain inactive. The family being intensely Southern in their political predilections, all possible aid and sympathy were given to Quantrell. Many dark nights Jesse would mount his best horse and ride through the gloomy wilderness of Western Missouri until he gained the guerrilla haunts, where he would deliver important information concerning the movements of Federal troops.

The part played by Jesse and the open and decided expressions frequently made by Dr. Samuels and his decidedly demonstrative wife, greatly excited the Federal soldiers, and it was determined to make an example of the family. Accordingly, in June, 1862, a company of Missouri militia approached the Samuels' homestead, which is near Kearney, in Clay county, and first meeting Dr. Samuels, they soon gave him to understand that their visit was made for a purpose decidedly unpleasant to him.

A strong rope was produced with which he was securely pinioned and then led away from the house a distance of about one hundred yards. Here the rope was fastened in a noose around his neck, while the other end was thrown over the limb of a tree, and several men hastily drew him up and left him suspended to choke to death. Mrs. Samuels, however, had followed stealthily, and the moment the militia had departed she rushed to the rescue of her husband, whom she hastily cut down, and by patient nursing saved his life. The enraged troops decided also to hang Jesse James, whom they found plowing in the field, but his youth saved him from

Hanging of Dr. Samuels.

any other violence than a few cuffs and the production of a rope with a suspicious noose which they threatened to ornament his neck with if he again visited the guerrilla camp.

Instead of producing the desired effect, this act of the militia only excited Jesse the more, and led him to deeds of graver importance. He continued to communicate almost daily with Quantrell, which so exasperated the militia that they paid a second visit to the Samuels' residence, decided upon killing both Dr. Samuels and the daring Jesse. When they reached the place, however, they found their intended victims absent, but, determined not to return without some trophy of their revengeful sortie, they took Mrs. Samuels and her daughter, Miss Susie, captive, and carried them to St. Joseph, where they were kept confined in jail for several weeks. This last act greatly inflamed Jesse's passions, and he immediately mounted his horse and again rode to Quantrell's camp, where, after detailing the particulars of this last outrage, perhaps exaggerating the facts some in order to make his appeal more effective, he begged the guerrilla commander to accept his services as a private. So hard did he plead for permission to join the ranks that marched under the shadow of the black flag, that at length the barrier which his youth imposed was overlooked and the terrible Quantrell oath was administered to him.

THE FIRST SKIRMISHES.

Up to this time the guerrillas had been engaged in but few skirmishes, their services consisting chiefly in small foraging expeditions, making themselves thoroughly acquainted with the topography of the country preparatory to engaging in more effective measures. There was a slight brush at Richfield, in which Captain Scott, with twelve of Quantrell's men, surprised thirty militia whom they captured, after killing ten, and in this attack Jesse James participated. Upon his return to camp he was sent out with orders from Quantrell to scour the counties adjoining Clay and locate the militia. After passing through Clinton county he paid a short visit to his mother, who received him with many manifestations of pleasure, and then began to unload herself of the valuable information she had gathered for the benefit of the guerrillas. She told him that the attack on Richfield had resulted in massing the militia for a determined stroke, and that the troops were concentrating near that point; that Plattsburg had been almost entirely relieved of its garrison and would fall an easy prey to the guerrillas if they chose to profit by the opportunity.

Jesse lost no time in communicating the situation to Quantrell, and, accordingly, three days after the capture of the squad of militiamen at Richfield, Captain Scott took fifteen men and silently stole upon Plattsburg, which he found defended by less than a score of Federals, under the command of a lieutenant. The guerrillas dashed into the town about 3 P. M. (August 25th), yelling like a tribe of Comanche Indians. The citizens fled into their houses with such fear that few ventured to look into the streets even through key holes. The Federal lieutenant chanced to be in the public square when the charge was made, and Jesse James had the honor and credit of capturing him. The rest of the militia gained the court-house, where it would have been impossible to dislodge them, and to have attacked the building would have exposed the guerrillas to the fire of the enemy. It was here that Jesse James' strategy and military tact were first manifested. Turning his prisoner (the lieutenant) over to Captain Scott, he said in a loud voice: "Captain, there is no use parleying with these cut-throats; shoot this fellow if he don't order his men in the court-house to surrender immediately." Captain Scott replied that he would if the court-house was not surrendered in two minutes. The result was that Plattsburg fell into the hands of the guerrillas, who pillaged the town and gathered booty, consisting of two hundred and fifty muskets, several hundred rounds of ammunition, ten thousand dollars in Missouri warrants, besides a large quantity of clothing, etc. The money was divided among the participating guerrillas, each of whom received nearly one thousand dollars in warrants besides clothing and other articles of value. The guerrillas compelled the landlord of the principal hotel to prepare them a good supper, to which they invited their prisoners, whom they paroled; and after feasting until 9 o'clock P. M., they withdrew to the cover of the forest.

After raiding Plattsburg, Quantrell broke camp and moved southward, passing through Independence, and bivouaced near Lee's Summit. The residents of that section suffered pitilessly from the sack and pillage of both Federals and Confederates. They occupied a middle ground which was subject to the incursions of both armies, and what was left after the forage of the Union forces was remorsely appropriated by the guerrillas. There were skirmishes almost daily, and every highway was red with human blood. The James boys, young as they were, became the terror of the border; the crack of their pistols or the whirr of their pirouetting bowies daily proclaimed the sacrifice of new victims. The sanguinary harvest grew broader as the sickle of death was thrust in to reap, and the little brooks and rivulets that had babbled merry music for ages and laved the thirst of man and beast with their crystal water, suddenly became tinged with a dye fresh from the fountain of bitterest sorrow. And thus the days sped on heavy with desolation. Quantrell and his followers were scarcely interrupted by the militia, who never attacked them except at the price of terrible defeat, until at length a direful scheme was proposed in which the desperate character of these free riders was manifested in its blackest hues.

THE DESOLATION OF LAWRENCE.

LAWRENCE, Kansas, a thrifty town located on the Kaw river, was selected by Quantrell as the place upon which to wreak a long-pent-up vengeance. Sitting around the camp fire on the night of August 18th, 1863, the chief of the black banner held a consultation with Frank and Jesse James, the Younger boys, the Shepherd brothers, and others of his most daring followers, as to the next advisable move upon a place which would furnish the best inducements for their peculiar mode of war. There was a concert of opinion that Lawrence was the most available place. The point having been selected, Quantrell did not neglect to inform his followers of the danger such an undertaking involved; that their road would be infested with militia, the forces of which would be daily augmented when the first intimation of the purposes of the guerrillas should be made known; that it would be ceaseless fighting and countless hardships, and many would be left upon the prairies to fester in the sun. He then called his command to arms and acquainted every man with the decision in the following speech: "Fellow soldiers, a consultation just held with several of my comrades has resulted in a decision that we break camp to-morrow and take up a line of march for Lawrence, Kansas; that we attack that town and, if pressed too hard, lay it in ashes. This undertaking, let me assure you, is hazardous in the extreme. The territory through which we must pass is full of enemies, and the entire way will be beset by well armed men through whom it will be necessary for us to carve our way. I know full well that there is not a man in my command who fears a foe; that no braver force ever existed than it is my honor to lead, but you have never encountered danger so great as we will have to meet on our way to Lawrence; therefore let me say to you, without doubting in the least your heroism, if there are any in my command who would prefer not to stake their lives in such a dangerous attempt, let them step outside the ranks."

At the conclusion of Quantrell's remarks a shout went up from every man, "On to Lawrence!" Not a face blanched, but on the other hand there was but one desire, to lay waste the city on the Kaw.

On the following day the order was given to "mount," and with that dreadfully black flag streaming over their heads the command, two hundred strong, turned their faces to the west. As they crossed the Kansas line at the small town of Aubrey, in Johnson county, Quantrell compelled three men, whom he found sitting in front of a small store kept by John Beeson, to accompany him as guides. The command passed through Johnson county midway between Olathe and Spring Hill, and through the northern part of Franklin county. When they reached Cole creek, eight miles from Lawrence, the three guides were taken into a clump of thick woods and shot by Jesse and Frank James. One of the party, an elderly man, begged piteously to be spared, reminding his executioners that he had never done them any wrong, but his prayers for mercy ended in the death rattle as a bullet went crashing through his neck.

Quantrell had been agreeably mistaken concerning the resistance he expected to encounter. Not a foe had yet appeared, but he never permitted a person to pass him alive. No less than twenty-five persons whom he met in the highway, after getting into Kansas, had been shot, and yet he avoided the public roads as much as possible.

Early in the morning of August 21st Quantrell and his band came in sight of the fated town. The sun was just straggling above the undulations of the prairie and the people of the place were beginning to resume the duties of a newly-born day. With a cry which froze the blood of every one in the town who heard it, Quantrell and his two hundred followers descended upon the place with pistol, sword and firebrand.

FLEEING FROM LAWRENCE.

The prime object of the guerrillas was to capture Gen. Jim Lane, who resided at Lawrence, and retaliate upon him for the burning and sacking of Osceola, Mo., which had been accomplished by men under his command. But Lane fled on the first alarm, and concealed himself in an adjacent cornfield. Foiled in their desire to capture him, the enraged guerrillas turned their vengeance loose upon the ill-fated town, killing every man who came within range of their deadly revolvers. Quantrell's orders were to kill all the men, but to spare the women and children. By accident, however,—possibly by design of some drunken privates—several women and children were shot; and this fact was made use of in subsequent reports of the affair to greatly exaggerate its barbarous details. It was certainly sufficiently inexcusable and barbarous without exaggeration. The torch was applied to the light frame buildings as the killing progressed, and the beautiful little city was soon enveloped in a sheet of flames. Stores and saloons were broken into and robbed of their contents, and the guerrilla band soon became a howling mob of drunken madmen. The dreadful harvest of death and destruction lasted nearly all day, and when the guerrillas took up their line of retreat toward the borders of Missouri, the city of Lawrence had disappeared from the face of the earth. In this affair Jesse James is said to have killed thirty men and Frank thirty-five. They seemed to take a sort of devilish pride in numbering their victims.

Quantrell and his men hastily retraced their steps, but they were terribly harassed during the entire return march by the Kansas militia and Federal troops that hurriedly concentrated and went in pursuit of them. This force has been reliably estimated at fully seven thousand, and nothing but hard marching, determined fighting, and an endurance that has never been equalled saved the guerrillas from total destruction. At Black Jack, about fifteen miles from Lawrence, a stand was made and some brisk fighting occurred. The guerrillas took to cover in a large barn which stood at the edge of an orchard. Several assaults were made to dislodge them but in vain. The horses of the guerrillas were suffering severely, however, and realizing that without horses they would be unable to get out of Kansas, the guerrillas made a desperate charge in which thirty-two of the militia were killed and a panic was the result. But the guerrillas did not care to follow up the victory, as every moment was precious. The militia were swarming and closing in upon them rapidly, and it was only by the rarest stroke of fortune that Quantrell and his men ever escaped from Kansas; this rare fortune was due entirely to the unparalleled cowardice of three hundred well armed and mounted men who had been organized into a militia force near Spring Hill, Kansas. These men exhibited remarkable bravery until the enemy appeared in sight, when they immediately retreated and never halted until they were ten miles from the place where they saw Quantrell. Had they engaged the enemy, which was one-third less in number, besides badly fatigued, they could either have beaten Quantrell or held him at bay until enough reinforcements were received to have annihilated every one of the guerrilla band.

It was a continual fight, however, and as Quantrell predicted, many of his followers were left dead and unburied on the hot prairies, where they became the prey of carrion birds. At Shawnee, in the northern part of Johnson county, the last stand was made, but the fight lasted only a few minutes, for the guerrillas, appreciating the critical position they occupied, with nearly five thousand militia gradually surrounding them, in the manner of early settlers who join in general hunts for the destruction of obnoxious wild animals, Quantrell soon ordered a charge and retreat. After breaking through the lines the guerrillas disbanded and each one then considered alone his own safety; this rendered a general pursuit impossible, and with a total loss of twenty-one men the bands reached the coverts of Jackson and Clay counties, where they were comparatively safe.

DESPERATE FIGHTING BY SQUADS.

After spending a month in apparent leisure, during which time Jesse and Frank James were frequent night visitors to their old home, Quantrell again called his command together for the purpose of resuming active hostilities, but he changed his tactics and added new terrors to the border counties of Missouri. The command was divided into squads of twenty and thirty, by which means they could make bold dashes at various points almost simultaneously and so confuse their enemies as to make pursuit futile. Indeed this peculiar and remorseless warfare gave rise to the strange superstition that Quantrell was some spirit of darkness who could transport himself and troops from place to place in the twinkle of an eye. He became no less dreaded by the Federal troops than by Union citizens, and day and night non-combatants as well as armed militiamen fell victims to the terrible guerrillas.

In the early part of October, Jesse James, in charge of a squad of twenty-five men, learning of the movements of a company of Federal cavalry under command of Capt. Ransom, who was marching toward Pleasant Hill, made a rapid detour and flanked the Federals five miles north of Blue Springs. Jesse selected a place near the road which was well screened by a dense thicket; here he stationed his men, and when the Federals came riding leisurely by, unconscious of any lurking danger, suddenly a storm of bullets poured upon them from the thicket and men fell like leaves in an autumn gust. The entire company was immediately thrown into the greatest confusion. The youthful commander of the guerrillas made the most of his advantage and ordered a dash into the confused and stricken ranks of the enemy, which he shot down with as little resistance as is offered by dumb animals. The havoc was terrible, for out of nearly one hundred Federals less than one-third the number escaped, while the loss of the guerrillas was only one killed and three slightly wounded.

On the following day another squad of Quantrell's men ambushed a body of militia who were returning from a forage in Lafayette county, and mercilessly annihilated nearly every one of the unfortunate command. One week later Frank and Jesse James, with fifty men, suddenly appeared in Bourbon county, Kansas, five miles south of Fort Scott, and swooped down upon Capt. Blunt and his company of seventy-five mounted infantry, and with a yell of rage and triumph swept with deathly missiles the astonished Federals, leaving forty of them to bleach in autumn rains.

The next attack was upon Lieut. Nash's command, three miles west of Warrensburg, Missouri, which was surprised by the guerrillas and cut to pieces. Following close upon this came the furious desolation of Camden. This little town was garrisoned by a small company of Federals, who, upon the day in question, were in the midst of bachanalian revels and unable to offer any resistance. This fight was a slaughter, in which the drunken soldiers were shot down without compunction, and the riot of murder was a pastime of sport for the guerrillas. After completing the harvest of death the town was pillaged and fired, and when the guerrillas rode out of the place they left its ruins in charge of the dead.

Another squad, under command of George Todd, suddenly encountered the Second Colorado cavalry, under command of Capt. Wagner, and a desperate fight ensued. The Colorado troops understood guerrilla warfare, and Wagner was as brave a man as ever mustered a company. The guerrillas made a furious charge, but the onslaught was met with such resistance that the opposing forces mingled together in a hand-to-hand contest. The fight was terrible, the rattle of revolvers being at times almost drowned by the clash of sabers. Jesse James fought like a hungry tiger, and his death-dealing pistol made terrible inroads among his foes. Singling out the Captain, who was fighting with wonderful desperation, Jesse rode by him at a furious pace, and, discharging his pistol with remarkable accuracy, he sent a bullet through the brave Captain's heart. This act sent consternation through the ranks of the Colorado troops, and a retreat, in confusion, was soon begun. Those that were wounded received no mercy at the hands of the guerrillas, but were shot or put to the sword and then left unburied.

Every attack made by the guerrillas added new terrors to the neighborhood; there was a concentrating of militia at every available point and a thousand schemes proposed by which to surprise and bring to punishment the desperate band; but the guerrillas were kept thoroughly posted and continued their reckless mode of warfare with varying success.

In the early part of 1864 Frank James was sent out by Bill Anderson to locate and number the Federal force at Harrisonville. The duty was fraught with much peril, but it was danger the James Boys courted as the spice of existence. He rode straight for the town, until within sight of the picket lines. He then hitched his horse in the closest thicket he could find, after which he approached with great care, and at night succeeded in passing the pickets. Very soon after reaching the outskirts of Harrisonville he met a negro from whom he obtained what information he desired and then crept back again through the lines and mounted his horse. At this juncture he was spied by two of the picket guards, who commanded him to halt. The reply came from his pistol, and though the night was without moonshine he sent a bullet through the brain of one, and another shot tore through the body of the other picket. The camp was speedily in arms but Frank rode rapidly out of harm and delivered the information he had gained with such risk to Anderson.

On the second day thereafter the plan of attack on Harrisonville was consummated and a hard fought battle was the consequence, but the guerrillas were forced to retire, and they turned their attention to a company of Federal volunteers who were encamped on Grand river at Flat Rock Ford. These they attacked with determined fierceness, but they were met with equal force and were again compelled to retreat. In this fight Jesse James was badly wounded, a musket ball having passed through his breast, tearing away a large portion of his left lung and knocking him from his horse. Notwithstanding the rain of bullets, Arch Clements and John Jarrette rode back, and gathering up their wounded comrade they bore him to the house of Capt. John M. Rudd, where for several days his death was hourly expected. Careful nursing and the best surgical skill, however, saved his life, and in one month's time he was able to resume the saddle, and in six weeks he again went on active duty.

On the 16th of September, 1864, Jesse James concluded to pay another visit to his mother, but the road thence was beset with a thousand dangers which very few men could be induced to encounter. During the ride he came suddenly upon three uniformed militia, who ordered him to halt, but instead of obeying the summons he whipped out two pistols and in a moment the three men were struggling in the throes of death. Jesse met with no other adventure on the journey, and after spending two days with his mother returned to the camp of the guerrillas. Immediately upon his return he was informed of the plans conceived during his absence, of attacking Fayette, Missouri. On the 20th the attack was made, and charge after charge, with all the force the guerrillas could command, was hurled against the stockades which protected the Federals, but every onslaught was firmly met and left a trail of dead and wounded guerrillas. Lee McMurtry, one of the bravest of Anderson's forces, fell dreadfully wounded directly un ler the Federal parapets. Jesse James was an intimate comrade of McMurty and he determined to rescue his friend. What a nature is that which can rush up to the very blazing muzzles of deadly rifles to drag away a wounded friend! But Jesse James seemed to court death without the ability to win it. He braved that lurid stream of fatal fire and drew away the gasping form of his friend, and yet escaped unscathed. This battle also resulted adversely to the guerrillas, and they were driven with great loss from Fayette. Leaving this place they rode west again and went into camp near Wellington.

DIREFUL MASSACRE AT CENTRALIA.

QUANTRELL continued to direct the movements of the guerrilla bands, but he was rarely engaged in any of the battles; the active service he delegated to the most strategical and unmerciful members of his command. Bill Anderson, a human tiger in disposition, was placed in charge of the full force when it was decided to move upon Centralia, a small town in Boone county, on the Wabash, St. Louis & Pacific Railway. On the 27th of September, one week after the attack on Fayette, the guerrillas, numbering one hundred and fifty men, headed by Anderson and that most ominous of banners, the black flag, with skull and cross-bones, marched upon Centralia, which they took possession of without resistance. After pillaging the place the guerrillas took up their station at the depot and awaited the coming of the train. They had not long to wait, for soon the shrill whistle of the engine, as it came thundering through a cut, drawing five passenger coaches loaded with soldiers and citizen travelers, announced the coming of the prize. The moment the train stopped the dreadful black flag was flung out and with the exchange of a few shots the messengers of death boarded the cars. Everyone on the train was ordered out and made to form in line, after which the thirty-two soldiers were separated from the other passengers and all disarmed. Now the breathless suspense, the terrible forebodings and the anxiety as to the fate that would be meted out to them! Every soldier was shot as unmercifully as if they had been **obnoxious beasts or poisonous snakes.** The passengers were relieved of whatever valuables they possessed, after which they were permitted to proceed on their journey.

In the afternoon of the same day and before the guerrillas had departed from Centralia, a body of Iowa volunteers, one hundred strong, under the command of Major J. H. Johnson, rode into the town and in the space of a few hours the two forces met and engaged in a terrible conflict. Again Jesse James, who was the best pistol shot in the guerrilla service, made a furious dash at Major Johnson and planted a pistol ball almost in the center of the brave Major's forehead. The guerrillas now rushed upon the terrorized volunteers with such resistless impetuosity that they broke in confusion. The fight became a massacre, and but very few of the brave volunteers escaped to convey to anxious friends the dreadful fate that had befallen their comrades. One of the militiamen had a very remarkable escape. Being badly wounded, in the early part of the fight, he remained unconscious, with the blood streaming from a saber gash in his head, until the foe had departed. When the fight was over the guerrillas went among the wounded and shot them with their revolvers, determined that not a soldier should escape. This single exception to the consummation of guerrilla vengeance was supposed to be dead, and he therefore escaped the crowning feature of that day's massacre. When consciousness was regained he found himself alone, among the dead bodies of his comrades, and his shouts for help brought to his assistance the services of a kind old negro woman who took him to her house and obtained surgical aid, so that in two week's time he was able to return home.

The result of the fight at Centralia was not such as brought great encouragement to the guerrillas; the victory they gained was at the cost of nearly fifty of their number, whom it would be impossible to replace, because men of their bold, reckless and desperate character are rarely to be found. It was therefore determined to again divide up into squads and renew the warfare which they had waged so successfully in the previous year. But the guerrillas never fought again as they had at Fayette and Harrisonville; their courage to meet an armed force seemed to have vanished.

FORTUNE TURNING AGAINST THE GUERRILLAS.

The numerous and desperate deeds of the guerillas received the earnest condemnation of the Confederate forces and for a time it was seriously considered, by many of the most distinguished Confederate officers, advisable to unite in the effort to rid Missouri of this terrible scourge. But their career was rapidly culminating. In attempting to cross the

Missouri river in Howard county, a detachment of the guerrillas, headed by Bill Anderson, was attacked by a force of Federals under Montgomery, and in the fight which ensued Anderson and five of his men were killed, while the others escaped to the hills. They were again surprised while in camp on the Blackwater and several more were killed, and Jesse James was badly wounded in the leg, besides having his horse killed under him. In another fight which followed soon after, on Sugar creek, George Todd, one of the most daring and shrewd of Quantrell's old comrades, was shot to the death, and in the latter part of 1864, in order to save themselves from capture or annihilation, the guerrillas concluded to disband finally. Jesse James joined his fortunes with George Shepherd and went to Texas, while Frank James followed Quantrell to Kentucky.

THE WHIRLWIND OF DESTRUCTION CHANGES.

IN January, 1865, Quantrell collected together nearly fifty of his old followers, among whom was Frank James, and started for the hills of Kentucky, where he expected to continue his warfare. Their route lay south-east, and before they got out of Missouri they came very near falling into the hands of Curtis, who pursued them hard almost to the Arkansas line, where the trail was lost. The guerrillas crossed the Mississippi river at Gaine's Landing, nearly twenty miles above Memphis, and made their way through Tennessee, entering Kentucky from the south. At Hartford, in Ohio county, the command met a squad of thirty militia under command of Capt. Barnett, whom they readily deceived into the belief that they were Federal troops searching for guerrillas, and that Quantrell was a Federal captain. Indeed the deception was played so successfully that Barnett was induced to accompany them upon an expedition. Quantrell managed to communicate with each of his men, whom he instructed to ride beside the Federals, and when he should draw his handkerchief and throw it over his shoulder it was the signal for the slaughter. At about five o'clock in the afternoon Frank James rode up beside Capt. Barnett, while Quantrell moved forward, and as his horse stepped into a shallow branch where all his men could see him, he drew the fatal handkerchief, and without looking back he waved it and then threw it over his shoulder. Their was a rattle of pistol shots and Capt. Barnett and his men fell dead under their horses.

Near Hopkinsville the guerrillas met twelve Federal cavalrymen who sought the shelter of a barn and gave battle. The fight lasted for more than an hour, and until the barn was fired, when the twelve brave fellows were forced from their defense and were shot as they rushed from the flames. Their horses then became the property of the guerrillas. Frank James stopped one day with an uncle, who lives about fifty miles from Hopkinsville, and thus permitted the command to get so far ahead of him that he did not engage in any more skirmishes in Kentucky; for, two days afterward, Quantrell was driven into a small village called Smiley, where, finding escape impossible, he made his last stand. It was forty against nearly three hundred, and Quantrell knew that it was a fight to the death. Bleeding almost at every pore, the black-bannered bandit fought like the gladiators, until, blinded by his own blood, and with a score of gaping wounds, he fell mortally wounded, with an empty pistol in one hand and a bloody sword in the other. It was thus that the entire force of Quantrell's guerrillas died, excepting Frank James, whose life was spared for darker deeds.

JESSE JAMES' CAREER IN TEXAS.

As previously stated, Jesse James left Missouri in company with George Shepherd and forty or fifty guerrillas, for Texas, where they spent the winter of 1864-5 without special activity, and in the spring it was decided to return to Missouri, although such a decision was pregnant with a renewal of all the dangers from which they had just escaped. Upon reaching Benton county Jesse James, Arch Clements and another comrade proceeded to the farm-house of James Harkness, who was known as an uncompromising Union man. They decoyed him a short distance from his house by requesting him to direct them to a spring which they knew was in the neighborhood. When out of sight of the house Jesse James and his comrade caught Harkness by the arms and held him firmly, while Arch Clements drew a large bowie-knife with which he cut the throat of the defenceless farmer, almost severing his head. Fresh blood being upon their hands, they rode into Johnson county to the house of Allen Duncan, another Union man, and finding him chopping wood in his yard, Jesse James first accosted him and then sent a bullet into his brain.

The guerrilla band, now numbering scarce a score, before getting out of Johnson county were surprised by a company of Federal volunteers and almost annihilated. Jesse James had his horse shot under him and a musket ball went crashing through his lungs. Supposing him dead, the Federals gave pursuit to the fleeing guerrillas and chased the remaining few for nearly fifty miles. The wounded guerrilla lay for two days where he fell, in terrible agony, and would have died except for the kindly ministrations of a farmer who chanced to find him. The care he received, after weeks of suffering, enabled him to again resume the saddle, and he went to Nebraska, where his mother was temporarily living and where he remained until the return of Frank James from Kentucky late in the following summer.

Before Frank left Brandensburg, however, he met with an adventure which nearly cost his life. The vicinity of Brandensburg was infested with horse-thieves, and suspicion was directed against Frank as one of the guilty band. It was determined to arrest him, and for this purpose a posse of six men went to the house where he was stopping, and after charging him with horse-stealing, demanded his arms. The response was most unexpected, for, with an oath, he drew his pistol and shot three of the party, and in return was badly wounded in the thigh. The other three fled, but a large crowd soon collected, to intimidate which Frank backed up against the house and threatened to shoot any one who made the least motion to harm him. A horse was standing hitched conveniently near, and, compelling the crowd to fall back, he drew his suffering body up into the saddle and made his escape. The wound proved a very serious one and kept him confined to his bed at the house of a friend, where he found refuge, nearly seventy-five miles from Brandensburg, for several months.

ROBBERY AND MURDER.

It is a trite old saying that "one crime begets another," and in the life of Jesse and Frank James it is well illustrated. When the war closed and the occupation of the guerrilla, under color of authority, was gone, the James Boys were loth to change the exciting and dangerous vocation to which they had become inured by nearly four years of almost ceaseless activity. Other guerrillas, who had been their comrades in so many desperate struggles, which had made their very names a terror, had surrendered themselves when the bond of national union had been repaired, and returned to peaceful pursuits; but Jesse and Frank James affected to despise the ordinary walks of life and refused to tread other than paths which bristled with danger and anxiety. Both were sorely wounded, and a period of recuperation was necessary; and this respite from the turmoils of bandit life was employed in the conception of bold schemes by which to enlarge the notoriety of their names and to accumulate wealth.

When they had somewhat recovered from their wounds, Mrs. Samuels returned to her old home, in Clay county, while the boys paid her occasional visits as opportunity offered, but generally keeping themselves well hidden in the fastnesses of Jackson county. In the latter part of 1866, Jesse James was attacked with a severe type of malarial fever, which the exposure he had to endure so intensified that he determined to secretly visit his mother and place himself under her immediate care. The record which he had made during the war rendered him amenable to the vengeance of a large number of the residents of Clay and adjoining counties, who had suffered by his desperate acts. Consequently, Jesse knew that eternal vigilance was necessary, but hoped to so conceal his presence at the Samuels' homestead that no one would suspect his location or condition. But in this he was deceived, for only a few days had elapsed after his arrival at home when, by some means unknown to the writer, it was discovered that Jesse had taken up at least a temporary residence with his mother.

It was a bitter cold night in the month of February, 1867, that a band of six persons, each of whom had a special grievance to revenge, knocked at the door of Dr. Samuels' residence and demanded immediate admittance. Jesse was in a bed up stairs, but he was the first to hear and understand the peremptory challenge, as it were, of the men outside. Hastily drawing on his pantaloons and boots, he grabbed his two heavy pistols and looked out of the window where, by the light refracted by the snow, he saw six horses and only a single man. He knew then that the house was surrounded and all chance of escape lay in a bloody fight. He silently descended to the first floor, where Dr. Samuels was rattling the door and explaining to those awaiting admittance that the lock was out of repair so that the key would not work readily. This was a ruse, however, to secure time for Jesse who, Dr. Samuels hoped, would be able to escape through a back window. Locating the voice of one of the men who was threatening to break in the door, Jesse fired through the panel and a stifled groan told him that his aim had been perfect. On hearing the shot, the other five rushed to the front of the house. Jesse threw the door partly open and the light from the snow made the men outside easy targets for his unerring aim, while he was so hidden by the door and darkness within that the attacking party could not fire with the least accuracy. In half the time it has taken the reader to even scan this report three of the six men were lying dead in the snow and two others were desperately wounded, while the other fled in mortal terror.

Suffering, as he was, from a very high fever, Jesse lost no time in mounting his horse, and with a hurried good-bye, he again rode into the wilderness, leaving his mother and her family with the dead and wounded. It was a ghastly scene, there upon the white-shrouded ground, one man dead on the doorstep, two others stiff and frozen in their own blood which crimsoned the yard, while the groans from the wounded made the place more hideous. Dr. Samuels notified his nearest neighbor as soon as possible

JESSE JAMES' RECEPTION.

and with the assistance he secured, the two wounded men were taken into the house and cared for, while a lonely vigil over the dead was kept until morning. A large crowd collected at the homestead on the following day and removed the bodies, while more than fifty well mounted citizens went in pursuit of the youthful desperado, but after a week's fruitless search they returned to their homes and quiet again brooded over the distressed neighborhood.

PLUNDERING A KENTUCKY BANK.

The bloody record of the James Boys had been almost forgotton, for they had not been seen in Clay county for many months and no specially reckless deeds had been committed to bring back a remembrance of them; when, suddenly, the town of Russellville, Kentucky, was thrown into a greater excitement than it had ever before experienced. The James Boys had paid the place a visit and left a souvenir of their desperate valor. On the 20th of March, 1868, Jesse James, accompanied by four comrades, George Shepherd, Oll. Shepherd, Cole Younger and Jim White, dashed into the town like a hurricane, yelling and firing their pistols until every one was frightened from the streets. They then rode to the bank where four of them dismounted and entered, with drawn revolvers, so intimidating the cashier that he opened the safe to Jesse James, while Cole Younger gathered the money that was lying upon the counter. The amount appropriated by the bandits was $14,000, which they threw into a sack and then leisurely departed. Everything connected with the robbery showed thorough system and a management which could be attributed to none other than the fierce Missouri free-booters.

When the excitement and surprise had somewhat subsided the sheriff summoned twenty deputies and started in pursuit. The chase continued through Kentucky and western Tennessee. Telegrams were sent in every direction with the hope of intercepting the robbers, who, finding themselves close pressed, scattered, as was their custom, and all, save George Shepherd, eluded pursuit and gained the marshes and dense coverts of Arkansas, where it was impossible to trail them. Shepherd was captured two weeks atter the robbery in a small drug store in Tennessee and taken back to Logan county, where he was convicted and sentenced to the penitentiary for a term of three years.

Oliver Shepherd, a brother of George, who was also connected with the bank robbery, was afterward found in Jackson county, Missouri, and a requisition being first obtained, a dozen men attempted his arrest. But Oll., as he was called, was made of that sterner composition which would not brook a curtailment of his liberty, and he threw defiance at the officers of the law. Then began a battle of extermination. The officers had armed themselves with carbines because they knew that to come in range of the old guerrilla's pistols would be death to many of them. The hero of a hundred desperate conflicts felt that his time had come, so, bracing himself against a large tree, he stood and received the fire of his slayers at a range of nearly two hundred and fifty yards. His pistols were useless, although he fired every shot, fourteen rounds, at the officers, who, from behind trees, shot seven terrible slugs into his body before he fell; even then, like Spartacus, he struck out towards his foes in the last throes of death.

BANK ROBBERY AND MURDER.

AFTER the affair at Russellville the James Boys appeared twice in their old haunts in Missouri, but spent nearly a year in Texas and Mexico, in remote districts, where they were free from the interference of officers anxious for their capture. It was not until the latter part of 1869 that they resumed criminal operations, their plans being laid to rob the bank at Gallatin, Missouri. In this scheme they were assisted by the three Younger brothers, whose career for consummate daring and recklessness is fully equal to that of the James Boys.

It was on the 7th of December that a body of

seven thoroughly armed men, superbly mounted, galloped into Gallatin and commenced firing their pistols indiscriminately, shouting most terrible oaths and fearful threats. After alarming the residents of the place and preventing resistance, Jesse James and Cole Younger dashed into the bank, and at the muzzles of drawn revolvers, they compelled the cashier, Capt. John W. Sheets, to deliver the keys of the money department of the safe, the main door being open. After rifling the bank of $700, Jesse and Cole whispered a few words together, put the money in a bag, and then one of them, but which of the two it is not known, deliberately shot Capt. Sheets dead. The reason given for the commission of this crime was that Capt. Sheets had, during the war, led a party of militia against the guerrillas, in which conflict Bill Anderson was killed, and that the killing of Sheets was in revenge for Anderson's tragic death.

Capt. Sheets was a very popular man in Gallatin and the surrounding neighborhood, and when the news of the terrible tragedy and robbery spread, nearly the entire county arose in arms and demanded the blood of the assassins. Several bands were organized and started in pursuit, each taking a different route, with the hope that one of them might be able to apprehend the bandits before they could get out of the county. One of these bands, numbering twelve citizens, overtook the robbers on the edge of Clay county and a running fight ensued, in which one of the citizens was wounded slightly and the horse of another killed. These casualties ended the pursuit and the bandits reached Jackson county in safety, where they disappeared.

THE MYSTERIOUS HIDING PLACE IN JACKSON COUNTY.

IN perusing books and newspaper articles recording the adventures of the James and Younger boys, the reader must have been impressed with the somewhat singular assertion that pursuit of the bandits generally ended by their sudden disappearance in Jackson county, Missouri. I will confess that I have often wondered how it was possible for a body of men to mysteriously disappear in a certain locality and thereby end a close pursuit. A gentleman who has been intimate with the James Boys for a period of nearly twenty years and with whom I am intimately acquainted, volunteered to me the long-wished-for information, which he gave as follows, omitting only the exact location. I will use his own words as nearly as possible:

"You know," said he, "that Jackson county is one of the most rugged and broken districts in Missouri; it not only abounds with bluffs, but also, in at least a few places, with almost impenetrable thickets, fit

ROMANTIC SCENERY NEAR THE MYSTERIOUS CAVE.

only for the abode of catamounts and foxes. One day I was riding through Jackson county, I will not tell you where, when suddenly I was confronted by Frank James. He greeted me cordially and then said: '——, I have every confidence in you and I know you would not betray us to save your right arm; therefore I invite you to our retreat; come with me!' I followed him in a bridle path for nearly a mile, when we came to a precipitous bluff, the base of which was completely hidden by a thick growth. There was an entrance between the growth and bluff, where any one would least suspect it, because, at the mouth are two bold rocks, which are apparently attached to the bluff itself; this delusion is accomplished by keeping the interstices filled with fresh brush so laid as to appear like a natural coppice. This passage-way leads about fifty feet, to a large fissure in the side of the bluff, resembling a vestibule; from this we stepped into a large cave, quite roomy enough to contain comfortably more than a score of men and horses. I was astonished at the completeness of the arrangement of things in the cave. There was a cooking stove, the pipe of which extended up and was lost in the top of the cave. Frank James told me that the smoke from the stove passed into a fissure of rock which evidently opened into another cave, as no smoke could ever be seen issuing from the bluff. He then took me over to another part of the cavern, where there was a clear spring of beautiful water, and over this was another fissure from which there was a cool draft of air which thoroughly ventilated the entire cave. I could see that many of the conveniences of the place were due to no little labor. A part of the cave was ceiled nicely with grooved pine lumber so as to prevent dampness, and in this division was a large heating stove, and about a dozen beds, all supplied with neat bedding. In the rear of the cave, which was, perhaps, one hundred feet deep by sixty broad, were twenty-one stalls for the horses, and over the stalls was a large feed bin filled with oats and corn, but no hay, as the latter was too bulky to convey readily into the cave. But what surprised me most was the means of defence. There was an arsenal of fire-arms and a magazine for ammunition, while the approach to the cave was commanded by a fierce, breech-loading ten-pound cannon, which was kept constantly loaded with buckshot, and looked out towards the entrance in such a way that one man could defend the place against a hundred, for a discharge of that cannon would sweep everything out of the passage. The place is absolutely impregnable, even if it could be found, which it would be exceedingly difficult to do.

"I would not have told you this except for the fact that the cave is now abandoned and may never be occupied again, but yet there is a certain obligation, from which I do not feel myself wholly relieved, that causes me to keep the location of the cave a secret.

Frank James is in the East, and Jesse James — well, I don't know what has become of him, but I hope he is living in safety and happiness, as I believe he is, because, with all their crimes, the James Boys have been good friends to me."

A TERRIBLE FIGHT IN MEXICO.

AFTER robbing the Gallatin bank, the James Boys left Missouri and went to Texas, where they remained a short time and then crossed the border into Mexico. It has been suspected that they drove a herd of cattle across the border with them, but of this there is no ready proof, and the crimes of some greasers may have been attributed to the bandits. In the month of May, 1860, Frank and Jesse James rode into Matamoras and, as there was a fandango advertised to take place at a public house on the night of their arrival, they decided to attend. Accordingly, when the night shadows fell, they paid the price of admission and entered the hall, which was rapidly filling up with swarthy senoritas and hidalgoes. From the belts of the latter protruded the glittering handles of bright, keen stilettos, in preparation for the affray which is always anticipated.

The dance began about eight o'clock, with much spirit, and the whirl of the graceful girls soon excited a desire on the part of Frank and Jesse to participate, although they were not familiar with the movements and figures of the Spanish dances. Nevertheless they essayed an attempt, which only served to excite the ridicule of the Mexicans who, by gesture and speech, went so far in their sport and mimicry of the outlaws that at length Frank James knocked down one of the boldest. This act came near proving disastrous to both the boys, for the moment the Mexican fell to the floor another powerfully built hidalgo struck Frank a blow on the cheek which sent him spinning into the laps of two girls who were seated on a bench awaiting partners. For a moment he was so stunned as to scarcely know what to do, but Jesse saw where his aid was most needed and the next instant the powerful Mexican fell with a bullet in his brain. A general fight then ensued in which Jesse and Frank rushed for the door, but their passage was impeded; so nothing remained for the boys except to clear a way by shooting those who stood before them. Frank received a thrust in the shoulder from a stiletto and Jesse's right fore-arm was punctured with a similar instrument, but the boys fired rapidly and with such effect that four Mexicans lay dead and six others were dreadfully wounded, some mortally. Jesse was the first to break through the doorway, and as he did so he turned at the very instant a dagger, in the hands of a strong Mexican, was directed at Frank's heart, but ere the hand fell to its purpose a bullet from Jesse's pistol entered the Mexican's eye and he dropped dead at Frank's feet, striking the dagger deep into the floor as he fell. This fortunate shot enabled Frank to escape from the building and as the Mexicans had no arms except stilettos, they were powerless to continue the fight, but many of them rushed to their homes to procure firearms and horses, and the place was swarming so rapidly with blood-craving hidalgoes and greasers that the only avenue of escape lay in the river. They accordingly rushed toward their horses which were hitched in the woods near by, but just before reaching them three powerful Mexicans suddenly sprang upon Frank James, who was a little in the rear, and attempted to bind him with a stout cord which they threw over his shoulders. Fortunately, in running he had picked up a large bludgeon which lay in his path, and shaking himself loose from the grasp of his assailants he laid about him so briskly with this formidable weapon that in a moment the three Mexicans lay stunned on the ground at his feet, then hastily joining Jesse, who had already mounted and was holding his horse for him, he sprang into the saddle, and putting spurs to their restless steeds they plunged boldly into the Rio Grande and swam to the other side, while the Mexicans were riding about in every direction trying to find the bandits whom they did not imagine would dare to take to the river.

The boys made good their escape, but the wounds they had received in the fight were of a most pain-

FRANK JAMES COMBAT WITH THREE MEXICAN'S.

ful nature and required careful attention. Frank's was the most severe, and had not Jesse bandaged it with the greatest skill the outlaw must have bled to death before obtaining medical aid, for one of the veins in his neck had been severed. The two reached Concepcion, a small town in Texas, about one hundred miles from Matamoras, where they remained in charge of a surgeon for nearly three months before their wounds had healed sufficiently to permit them to travel.

PLUNDERING AN IOWA BANK.

In the spring of 1871 Jesse and Frank James secretly returned to their haunts in Jackson county, Missouri, where they remained for some time arranging for an expedition into Iowa. Their plans being perfected, they, with five other bandits, started north, riding by night, until they reached Corydon, the bank in which place they had previously decided to rob. At ten o'clock in the morning the seven desperadoes made a furious charge into the center of the town and commenced a fusilade of firing, threatening to kill every person found on the streets within five minutes afterward. None of the citizens thought of offering any resistance, and dashing up to the bank, three of the robbers dismounted and rushed in with cocked pistols, and demanded of the cashier every cent the bank contained. Finding himself powerless, and realizing that death would be his certain portion if he refused to comply with the immediate demands of the desperate outlaws, the cashier opened the safe and permitted them to appropriate nearly $40,000. The money was placed in a sack, which they invariably carried with them for the purpose, and then the seven desperadoes rode rapidly out of the city, firing their pistols indiscriminately as they swept through the streets.

The citizens were, of course, intensely excited, and after the disappearance of the robbers a hundred persons volunteered their services to the sheriff to assist in the apprehension of the bold plunderers. Efforts at capture were made by a large body of men, but like all similar attempts, the result was nothing. They were followed into Missouri and telegrams sent to every town in the State, but, like imps of darkness, the seven dare-devils disappeared and were not again seen for several months; but it is now known that they were lying quietly in their impregnable haunt in the eastern part of Jackson county, waiting for a return of quiet.

ANOTHER BANK ROBBERY IN KENTUCKY.

In the latter part of 1870, Jesse and Frank James visited Kentucky, where they had a large number of friends and relatives, who admired their bravery and condoned their crimes. They remained here until in the early part of the spring of 1874, when they and the Younger boys conceived a plan for robbing the bank at Columbia, Kentucky. On the 29th of April of that year, the three Youngers and the two James Boys entered Columbia about the same hour from five different roads, so that there was not the least apprehension excited. Just before three o'clock in the afternoon the five desperadoes rode up to the bank together, while Frank James and Cole Younger leisurely dismounted and entered the bank, where they found the cashier, Mr. Martin, the president, Mr. Dalrymple, and another gentleman engaged in a conversation. Without losing any time or creating any suspicion from the citizens of the place, the two bandits drew their pistols and going behind the bank counter, leveled them at the heads of the cashier and president, and demanded the keys to the safe. Seeing, at a glance, however, that the safe was secured by a combination lock, they commanded the cashier to open it under penalty of immediate death if he refused. Martin was a brave man, and instead of being intimidated, tried to raise an alarm; but at the first outcry Frank James thrust a heavy navy revolver into his face and fired, killing him instantly; at the same moment Cole Younger fired at the president but, luckily, that gentleman struck up the pistol, and running into the back office, escaped with his life. The two robbers hastily gathered the money that was in sight, (about $200,) and gaining their horses the five rode out of the town at a rapid pace.

Fifteen men, headed by the sheriff, went in pursuit of the desperadoes, and chased them hard into the eastern part of Tennessee, where the trail was lost in the Cumberland range. Again the bandits doubled on their tracks, after the pursuit was abandoned, and went into the western part of Texas, where they mingled with the lawless elements of the border.

Every attempt at their capture had proven fruitless, and for the time being, the provincial banks were kept well armed in anticipation of a raid. The James Boys were too crafty to appear again in the counties where their terrible deeds had excited the people to desperation. They waited until the memory of their crimes had been partially forgotten, and then planned new schemes of pillage.

ROBBING OF THE CASH-BOX AT THE KANSAS CITY FAIR.

ON the 26th of September, 1872, the people of Kansas City had an opportunity for considering the cunning and bravery of the James Boys, from immediate circumstances which suddenly involved the city in a furore of excitement. It was on Thursday, the "big day" of the Kansas City Exposition, when nearly thirty thousand visitors were assembled to see the races, and particularly to witness Ethan Allen trot in harness against a running mate. The crowd was immense and of course the gate receipts were correspondingly large. About four o'clock in the afternoon Mr. Hall, the secretary and treasurer of the association, counted up the receipts of the day, which were nearly ten thousand dollars, and placing the money in a tin box kept for the purpose, he told one of his assistants to take it to the First National Bank where, although it was after banking hours, arrangements had been made to make the deposit. No thought was entertained that any attempt would be made to steal the cash-box while so many people were constantly on the highway leading to the city, and the young man started off whistling gaily, carrying the treasure box by a wire handle in his right hand. As he reached the entrance gate, where more than a dozen persons were coming in and going out, three men on horseback (Jesse and Frank James and Bob Younger) dashed up to the young man with such reckless haste that a little girl was badly trampled by one of the horses; at the same moment a pistol shot was fired and Jesse James jumped from his horse into the confused crowd and snatching the cash-box from the hand of the affrighted messenger, he leaped into the saddle again and the three highwaymen disappeared, with a clatter of fast-flying feet, like the sweep of a whirlwind. For several minutes it was thought that the little girl had been struck by a pistol ball, but after she was carried home it was ascertained that her injuries, which were not fatal, were caused by the horse of one of the robbers knocking her down and trampling upon her hips.

The news of the robbery spread over the city in a few minutes, and Marshal Shepherd sent out some of his detectives, while several gentlemen mounted fleet horses and used every possible endeavor to capture the robbers. The trail led over the hills east of Kansas City and about ten miles into Jackson county, where every trace was suddenly blotted out. The outlaws had reached their favorite haunt where no pursuer had ever been able to find them. The writer was a reporter on the Kansas City *Journal* at the time of the robbery and reported the details as here related.

PLUNDERING THE STE. GENEVIEVE BANK.

THE success of the bandits thus far greatly encouraged them in their lawless operations, and they were constantly planning new and still more reckless adventures. They remained in their secure hiding place during the winter of 1872-3, retiring upon their laurels and living royally upon their immense gains. During this period of jolly hibernation, schemes were proposed for wrecking railroad trains, and before the appearance of spring, Frank James and Jim Younger were sent into Nebraska for the purpose of

RECRUITING AFTER A RAID.

gathering information concerning the express shipment of treasure from the west. Not hearing from the robber agents as soon as was expected, Jesse James, Bill Chadwell, Clell Miller, and Bob and Cole Younger decided to pay their respects to another bank before venturing upon their proposed railroad enterprise, and the Savings Association, at Ste. Genevieve, Missouri, was selected for the strike. Accordingly, early in the morning of May 27th, 1873, the five desperate free-booters appeared in the streets of that old-time Catholic town, and the moment that Mr. O. D. Harris, the cashier, accompanied by F. A. Rozier, a son of Hon. Firman A. Rozier, the president, entered the bank to begin the business of the day, the three daring bandits followed them into the building and presenting six pistols, demanded the immediate opening of the bank vault. Young Rozier, regardless of the danger, made a speedy exit, and as he ran down the street crying for help, a bullet from one of the outlaws' weapons went whistling through the tail of his coat, but he escaped. Mr. Harris, however, was covered by too many pistols to permit of his escape, and stern necessity forced him into a compliance with the wishes of the robbers. He opened the vault, from which the sum of four thousand one hundred dollars was taken, a large part of which was specie, and shoving it speedily into the sack provided, the bandits mounted their horses and decamped. As they were riding out of the city, the bag containing the treasure was accidentally dropped, to recover which it was necessary to return, and one of the robbers had to dismount. In doing so his horse became frightened and broke away. At this juncture a German came riding by and the robbers compelled him to ride after and catch the fleeing animal, which was returned to the riderless bandit, only after such delay as permitted a hastily organized posse of the citizens to approach within pistol shot of the three highwaymen. An exchange of fire caused the posse to check their pace and the distance thus gained by the pursued was never made up. The pursuit was continued for several days, but without result. The outlaws stopped at Hermann, Mo., two days after the robbery, but as usual, there was no posse there to apprehend them. Several well known detectives from St. Louis were sent out, and the sheriff of every county in Missouri notified and requested to keep a sharp lookout for the desperadoes; but though many suspicious characters were arrested the real culprits were never captured. The amount secured at Ste. Genevieve was a great disappointment to the robbers, for it was known that the bank usually carried from seventy-five thousand to one hundred thousand dollars, but at this particular time, very fortunately, the association was winding up business, and had deposited the greater portion of its funds in the Merchants' Bank of St. Louis.

WRECKING AND PLUNDERING A TRAIN.

In June following both the James Boys were seen in Kansas City by intimate acquaintances, and the night of June 27th was spent by both the bandits with their mother at the Samuels' residence. On the 15th of July, Bob, Jim and Cole Younger, Jesse and Frank James, Bud Singleton and two other bandits, whose names have never been learned by the authorities, left Clay county, Missouri, and rode northward to a spot which had been selected by Frank James and Jim Younger, on the line of the Chicago, Rock Island & Pacific Railroad, about five miles east of Council Bluffs. The reason for selecting this place and time was because of information received of an intended shipment of a large amount of gold from San Francisco to New York, which would be made over this route, reaching Omaha about the 19th of July. How this information was imparted was never ascertained, but its truth has led to the belief that the James Boys had confederates on the Pacific slope with whom they were in constant communication.

On the evening of July 21st a formidable band of eight of the most desperate men that ever committed a crime, took position in a dense thicket beside a deep cut in the railroad. They hitched their horses out of view of passengers on the train and then, after a few minutes' work, displaced one of the rails. This accomplished, they waited the coming of the express train which was due at that point at 8:30 P. M. From a knoll near the rendezvous Jesse James descried the blazing headlight of the coming train, and then made everything ready for their villainous work. A sharp curve in the track prevented the engineer from discovering anything wrong, until it was impossible to prevent the disaster which the banditti had prepared for. The screaming engine came thundering like an infuriated mammoth, which a reversal of the lever only began to check when it struck the loosened rail and plunged sideways into the bank, while the cars telescoped and piled up in terrible confusion. The engineer was instantly killed, and a dozen passengers were seriously injured, but the desperadoes did not stop to consider this terrible disaster. The moment the havoc was complete the bandits fell upon the excited passengers, whom they robbed without exception, both men and women, taking every species of jewelry and the last cent that could be discovered from the wounded as well as those who remained unhurt. The express car was entered and the messenger, groaning with pain from a broken arm, was compelled to open the safe, which was rifled of six thousand dollars and then the messenger was forced to give the robbers his watch and ten dollars which he had with him. Fortunately the desperadoes were twelve hours too soon for the train upon which the expected treasure was carried, as the express that went east on the morning of the 21st, carried gold bricks, specie and currency amounting to over one hundred thousand dollars.

The total amount secured by the train-wrecking band was about $2,500 each, which they carried off, as was their custom, in a sack, departing southward at a rapid gait.

The officers of Council Bluffs were soon notified of the robbery. The wounded and dead were taken to the city and cared for, and then another pursuit of the robbers was begun, which was united in by sheriffs and posses of other counties until the pursuing parties numbered nearly two hundred men. The desperadoes were traced over hill and prairie, through Clay county and into Jackson, where the trail was lost as effectually as if the robbers had mounted into space and fled behind the clouds. Reward after reward was offered until they aggregated more than $50,000; the most expert detectives from St. Louis and Chicago concentrated upon an effort to win the prize and rid the country of the most consummate highwaymen since the days of Rolla, the bearded Knight of the forests. But every clue proved deceiving, and the most cunning of detectives finally abandoned the chase, thoroughly confounded by the marvelous cunning of the bandits.

THE STAGE ROBBERY NEAR HOT SPRINGS.

In December of 1873, a council was held in the haunt of the bandits, near the Big Blue, in Jackson county, in which it was decided to attempt a stage robbery, and the line between Malvern and Hot Springs, Arkansas, was selected for the first stroke in the inauguration of a new species of crime. Accordingly, on the 15th of January, 1874, five of the highwaymen, consisting of Frank James, Clell Miller, Arthur McCoy and Jim and Cole Younger repaired to the scene of their intended operations and secreted themselves in a dense covert on the south side of the stage road, five miles from Hot Springs, and awaited the coming of their victims.

The conception of this scheme manifested the judgment of the bandits, for they were influenced by the supposition that those who visited Hot Springs in search of health, were people of liberal means who would naturally carry with them a goodly sum of money with which to meet expected large expenses, and in this their judgment was correct.

It was after mid-day when the heavy Concord stage, filled with passengers, came rattling over the rough and stony road opposite the secret hiding place of the highway freebooters. Suddenly a shot startled the driver, and his surprise culminated when Jesse James arose from a clump of brush, and with a heavy revolver in each hand, commanded the driver to halt. The order was instantly obeyed, and as the passengers thrust their heads out of the vehicle they saw five fierce looking men, armed and spurred, whose purposes were at once divined. Frank James, who acted as leader, ordered the occupants of the stage to get out, which being complied with the passengers were formed into line and then submitted to a search by Clell Miller and Jim Younger, while the three other bandits stood guard with cocked pistols. The fright of the travelers was greatly intensified by the blood-chilling threats of the desperadoes. They jested with one another and made banters to test their skill as pistol shots on the trembling and unarmed passengers. "Now," said Frank James to Cole Younger, "I will bet you the contents of that fellow's pocket-book," pointing to one of the travelers who was a small tradesman at Little Rock, "that I can shoot off a smaller bit out of his right ear than you can." "I'll take the wager," responded Cole, "but you must let me have the first shot, because my eyesight is not as good as yours, and if you should hit his ear first the blood might confuse my aim." Frank insisted on shooting first, and in the wrangle, the poor victim trembled until he could scarcely retain his feet, and with the most prayerful entreaties begged the robbers to take what he had but spare his life.

Mr. Taylor, of Massachusetts, a sufferer from rheumatism, then drew the attention of the bandits, and Jesse James offered to bet his share of the booty that he could throw his bowie-knife through Taylor's underclothing without drawing blood. It was thus the bandits jested with one another and in turn had each of the fear-stricken passengers praying for his life.

When the search was concluded, Frank James produced a memorandum book and took the names of all the travelers, saying: " I am like lightning, I don't want to strike the same parties twice."

The total amount of money and valuables taken approximated $4,000, the heaviest loser being Ex-Gov. Burbank, of Dakota, from whom the robbers secured $1,500. When the bandits left their victims, they graciously and with great punctilio, raised their hats and bade them a most courteous adieu, wishing them a pleasant visit at the Springs.

When the travelers reached Hot Springs they were in a sorry plight, not one of them having enough money to send a message home for additional funds, but the citizens kindly provided for their wants and exhibited much sympathy, but little or no attempt was made to capture the highwaymen. Indeed any such effort would have undoubtedly terminated fruitlessly, for, in addition to the cunning and bravery of the bandits, the mountainous nature of the country would have prevented a pursuing party from making up the time lost in reporting the circumstances of the robbery.

THE TRAIN ROBBERY AT GAD'S HILL.

After leaving the scene of their Hot Springs adventure the five daring highwaymen, finding that they were not pursued, rode up into the northern part of Arkansas, where they had several friends, and there planned a scheme for plundering a train on the Iron Mountain Railroad. The place chosen for the purpose was Gad's Hill, a very small station in Wayne county, Missouri, which, in the summer time, is almost hidden by the copse of pine trees which surrounds it. The adjacent country was a very jungle in which it was easy to hide and elude the most determined pursuit.

On the last day of January, 1874, but little more than two weeks after their last successful robbery, the five bandits, with Frank James still acting as leader, rode into the station and made prisoners of every man in the place, consisting of the railroad agent, a saloon-keeper, blacksmith, two wood-choppers, and the son of Dr. John M. Rock. These were confined in the station house under threats of instant death if any attempt at escape were made. Having prevented every means of alarm, the desperadoes turned the switch in order to ditch the train if it attempted to run past, (as Gad's Hill was only a flag station,) and then planted a red flag in the track immediately in front of the station house.

The train was not due until 5:40 in the evening, at which time the shadows of twilight curtained the little place and prepared the approach of darkness. Promptly upon time the train came bowling along, and the engineer, seeing the danger-signal ahead, brought the engine to a standstill alongside the station house. No one was seen when the train stopped, but in a moment thereafter Cole Younger mounted the cab and, with drawn pistol, compelled the engineer and fireman to leave the engine and walk out into the woods. Mr. Alford, the conductor, was arrested by Jesse James as he stepped from the train to ascertain the cause of the display of the red flag. He was forced to give up his watch and $75.00 in money, after which he was placed in the station house. Then began a sack of the passengers. Clell Miller, Jim Younger and Frank James searched the affrighted people in the cars, while Jesse James and Cole Younger, taking opposite sides of the train, maintained a watch and kept shooting in various directions, while they uttered terrible oaths and threats, to keep the passengers in a state of constant trepidation.

After stripping all the passengers of every bit of valuables, the outlaws proceeded to the express car, where they broke open the safe and secured the contents. The mail car was next plundered and the letters cut open, one of which contained $2,000, and several smaller sums were obtained. The total amount of booty secured by the bandits was about $11,500. Having again successfully accomplished their criminal purpose without meeting any resistance, the five desperadoes released those confined in the station house; the engineer and fireman were recalled from their position in the woods, and the train was ordered to proceed. Then mounting their horses, which were hitched near by, the outlaws rode into the brush and disappeared in the darkness.

When the train reached Piedmont information of the robbery was telegraphed to Little Rock, St. Louis, and all the towns along the road. On the following day, a large body of well-armed men started from Ironton and Piedmont in pursuit of the desperate outlaws, and soon got on their track. The pursuing party found where the bandits had breakfasted, sixty miles from Gad's Hill; following the trail closely on the second day the citizen's posse reached the spot where the outlaws had spent the night, and they were encouraged by the belief that a capture might be effected before the close of the day, but suddenly the party came to a low marsh through which it was dangerous to ride, and in searching for a pathway around the boggy district much time was lost and the trail of the robbers could not be found again; so the pursuit was abandoned.

WICHER'S UNFORTUNATE HUNT FOR THE JAMES BOYS.

In the spring of 1874 John W. Wicher of Chicago, a brave, cool, cunning man, scarcely thirty years of age, connected with the Pinkerton force, appeared before his chief and asked to be sent out to discover the hiding place of the terrible brigands. He was fully informed of the dangers of such a mission, but his self-reliance and pride made him anxious to make the attempt which had already cost the lives of so many courageous officials. The chief gave his consent, and Wicher set out at once for the Samuels residence. In the early part of March the detective arrived in Liberty, where he soon laid his schemes before the sheriff of Clay county, and asked for assistance when the time and circumstances were ripe for a strike. The sheriff promised all needful aid and gave Wicher all the information in his possession concerning the habits and rendezvous of the James and Younger boys.

Changing his garb for the habit of a tramp, Wicher left Liberty on the 15th of March and arrived at Kearney on the same day, late in the afternoon. He took the road leading directly to the Samuels residence and had proceeded perhaps two miles on the lonely highway, when suddenly Jesse James walked out from behind a pile of dead brush and, with pistol presented, confronted the detective. Wicher's surprise was complete, but he manifested not the least excitement, his cool self-possession never deserting him for a moment.

"Where are you going?" was the first remark made by Jesse James.

"I am looking for work," was Wicher's reply.

"What kind of work do you want, and where do you expect to find it?" asked Jesse, his pistol still pointing full in poor Wicher's face.

"I have been used to farm labor, and hope to find something to do on some farm in the vicinity," responded the detective.

Jesse James smiled contemptuously and then gave a sharp whistle, which brought to his side Clell Miller and Frank James, whose near presence Wicher had not thought of. The conversation then continued. Said Jesse:

"You don't look much like a laborer, nor is there any appearance of a tramp about you except in your clothes. Now I want you to acknowledge frankly just what your purpose is in this part of the country."

The detective began to realize how critical was his position, and that unless the most fortuitous circumstance should arise in his favor his chances of escape were exceedingly small. But with the same coolness he made reply:

"Well, gentlemen, I am nothing more than a poor man, without as much as a dollar in my pocket, and what I have told you as to my purpose is true. If you will be good enough to let me proceed, or furnish me with means by which I can secure work I shall be thankful."

At this the bandits laughed scornfully, while Jesse James proceeded with the examination: "I think you are from Chicago, and when you arrived at Liberty a few days ago you wore much better clothes than you now have on; besides, it seems that you and Moss (the sheriff) had some business together. Say, now, young fellow, haven't you set out to locate the James Boys, whom you have found rather unexpectedly?"

Wicher then saw that he was in the hands of his enemies, and his heart beat in excited pulsations as he thought of the young wife he had so recently wedded, and from whom an eternal separation appeared certain. Dropping his head as if resigning himself to cruel fate, Wicher hoped to deceive his captors, and in an unguarded moment be able to draw his pistol and fight for his life. Like a flash from a hazy cloud, the detective thrust his hand into his bosom and succeeded in grasping his pistol, but ere he could use it the bandits sprang upon him, and in the grip of three strong men he was helpless. He was then disarmed and firmly bound by small cords which Frank James produced. Clell Miller went into the woods and soon returned leading three horses, on the largest of which Wicher was placed and his feet tied under the horse's belly. A gag was placed tightly in his mouth and Jesse James, mounting behind, the desperadoes rode into the deepening twilight of the woods with their victim. They crossed the Missouri river at Independence Landing, and just before day they halted in the black shadows of a copse in Jackson county. Here they prepared for the punishment and execution of their prisoner. Wicher was taken from his horse and bound fast to a tree; the gag was removed from his mouth and then the bandits tried to extort from him information concernihg the plans of Pinkerton and the number and names of the detectives he had engaged in the attempt to capture the outlaws. Though they pricked him with their bowie-knives and bent his head forward with their combined strength until the spinal column was almost broken, and practiced other atrocious torments, yet Wicher never spoke. He knew that death was his portion and he defied the desperadoes and dared them to do their worst. Finding all their endeavors fruitless, Jesse and Frank James murdered their victim; one of them shooting him through the heart and the other through the brain. The body was then carried to the nearest highway, where it was left to be found next day by a farmer who was driving into Independence.

MURDERING COW-BOYS AND DRIVING OFF CATTLE.

The excitement following the murder of Wicher was so great that the James Boys, Clell Miller, Arthur McCoy, and the three Younger brothers quit Missouri and again visited Texas. After carousing around through the State until their pecuniary means were well nigh exhausted, they determined upon the commission of a new crime, stealing a herd of cattle. It was in September, 1874, that the seven brigands rode into the southwestern part of the State, where they selected a herd of five hundred of the finest beef cattle in Starr county, which were being tended by three cow-boys. The herders were cruelly murdered and the robbers drove the cattle rapidly toward Mexico with the design of selling them to the Mexicans who cared little for the real ownership of the cattle after they were upon Mexican soil. On the extensive plains of Texas where the large herds are left in charge of cow-boys to roam from season to season, subsisting entirely upon the rich grasses of the prairies, the owners often do not see their cattle for months, trusting them to the care of the herders. It is due to this fact, perhaps, that the bandits, after killing the cow-boys, were permitted to drive the herd over sixty miles and into Mexico without being pursued.

Reaching Camargo the bandits had no difficulty in disposing of the cattle, and with this money they went on a big spree, which terminated in a fight with fifteen gringos, who were saloon loafers and petty disturbers by profession. The result of this combat was the wounding of Clell Miller and Jim Younger and the killing of two Mexicans. The bandits would have fared much worse, however, had they not gained their horses and made rapid retreat, gaining the Rio Grande so far in advance of their pursuers as permitted them to cross the river before the Mexicans reached the bank.

The free-booters having eluded their pursuers stopped at Camp Hudson for several weeks, where the wounds of Miller and Younger were attended to, and in December the party returned to Missouri, thinking that, as had been usual, the excitement over their crimes had so far subsided as to permit them to visit their old homes and haunts. Their appearance in Clay county, at least the James Boys, was noted on the 20th of January, 1875, and report of their return was at once made to Allen Pinkerton, who, after some correspondence with county officials and others, formed a plan for capturing the outlaws.

THE ATTACK ON THE SAMUELS RESIDENCE.

WILLIAM PINKERTON, a brother of the chief detective, was sent to Kansas City immediately with five of the most trusted men in the force. Upon arriving at that place the sheriff of Clay county was sent for, after which twelve citizens of known pluck and reliability were engaged to watch the Samuels homestead and report from hour to hour by a rapid means of communication, which had been established. The greatest secrecy was enjoined upon all engaged in the undertaking and every possible precaution was taken to prevent any alarm reaching the bandits.

On the afternoon of January 25th, Jesse and Frank James were both seen in the yard fronting the Samuels residence and report of this quickly reached the sheriff and Mr. Pinkerton who were in Liberty. Arrangements were made for the immediate capture of the two bandits, who it was confidently supposed would spend the night in their mother's house. Accordingly the two officers rode to Kearney late in the afternoon, where they organized a party of twelve men who were to assist them, and preparing several balls of cotton saturated with turpentine and two hand-grenades, the well armed body of men proceeded to the Samuels residence, which they reached about midnight. A reconnoissance was first made with great care for indications of possible surprise, and after completely surrounding the house four of the men, with turpentine balls, were sent forward to open the attack. A window on the west side of the residence was stealthily approached, but in the act of raising it an old colored woman, who had for many years been a house servant in the family, was awakened, and she at once gave the alarm. But the window was forced up and the two lighted balls were thrown into the room, and as the flames shot upward, threatening destruction to the house and its contents, the family were speedily aroused and efforts were made to extinguish the fire. At the moment every member of the household, consisting of Mr. and Mrs. Samuels, a son eight years of age, and the daughter, Miss Susie, and the old colored woman, had partially subdued the flames, one of the detectives, or at least one of the party leading the attack, flung a hand-grenade into the room among the affrighted occupants, and a heavy explosion was the prelude to the dreadful havoc made by that instrument of death. A scream of anguish succeeded the report and groans from within, without any evidence of the outlaws' presence, convinced the detectives and citizen's posse that they had committed a grave and horrible crime; so, without examining the premises further the party withdrew, apparently with the fear that the inexcusable deed they had just committed would be avenged speedily if they tarried in the vicinity.

When the lamp was lighted by Dr. Samuels he found his little boy in the agonies of death, having received a terrible wound in the side from the exploded shell. Mrs. Samuels' left arm had been shattered, and hung helpless by her side; but she forgot her own misfortune in the anguish she suffered at seeing the dying struggles of her little boy. What a terrible night was that memorable 25th of January to the Samuels family! Alone with their dead boy, whom they worshipped, and with a desperately wounded mother, who would certainly have bled to death but for the thoughtfulness of the old colored servant who hastily bandaged the arm and staunched the flow of the crimson life-current.

The funeral of the innocent victim did not take place until the second day after the midnight attack, and then Mrs. Samuels, who had suffered an amputation of the injured member, was too greatly prostrated to attend and witness the last service over her darling boy, but the remains were accompanied to the grave by a very large body of sympathizing people of the neighborhood.

This unfortunate and indefensible attack, for a time allayed public animosity against the James Boys and turned the sympathy of people in western Missouri somewhat in their favor. Those who had been most earnest in their desire to see Jesse and Frank James brought to punishment, began to think more lightly of their crimes, attributing them partly, at least, to the manner in which they had been hunted and persecuted. It is a notorious fact that for some time this sentiment predominated in Clay and Jackson counties, and the same feeling extended to other parts of the State, and in March following led to the introduction of an amnesty bill in the Legislature, granting immunity for past offenses committed by Jesse and Frank James, Coleman Younger, James Younger and Robert Younger. The bill was introduced by Gen. Jeff. Jones, of Callaway county, and contained a provisional clause that amnesty would be granted the parties named in the instrument for all offenses committed during the war, provided they would surrender to the lawful authorities and submit to such proceedings as might be brought against them in the several States for crimes charged against them since the war. After a stormy debate the bill was defeated, although had it passed none of the bandits named would have accepted the terms, for surrender meant either execution or life imprisonment. A rejection of the terms of surrender, by the Legislature, afforded a fresh pretext, however, to the bandits to pursue their crimes of blood and pillage, and it was not long before the country was again startled by the daring deeds of the outlaws.

ASSASSINATION OF DANIEL ASKEW.

IMMEDIATELY after the defeat of the "outlaw amnesty bill," as it was called, the brigands planned the execution of new and direful schemes, one of which involved the assassination of a respectable citizen of Clay county.

The James Boys concluded, for reasons known only to themselves, that Mr. Daniel Askew was a member of the posse which made the attack on the Samuels residence, and this belief was justification sufficient, in their estimation, for murdering that gentleman; but the plan of its execution was equally as dastardly as the casting of the hand-grenade blindly and savagely among the several members of Dr. Samuels' family. The circumstances of the assassination were as follows: Mr. Askew was an unpretentious farmer, living about five miles from Liberty, in a neat frame house, but with no neighbors nearer than one mile. He had returned home from Liberty, late in the afternoon of April 12th, 1875, and after eating supper took a bucket and went to the spring, which was fifty yards from the house, after water. This was about eight o'clock in the evening, but the moon was shining brightly and objects were plainly discernible. He returned from the spring with the water and sat the bucket upon a shelf on the porch, after which he proceeded to take a drink, but as he was in the act of lifting the cup to his mouth, three sharp shots rang out upon the still air and Mr. Askew plunged forward on his face dead, the three bullets having taken fatal effect upon his person, one entering the brain and the two others reaching vital spots in his body.

At the sound of the shots and the heavy fall on the porch, Mr. Askew's wife and daughter rushed out of the house just in time to see three men steal out from behind the cover of a large woodpile in front of the porch, and regain their horses and ride swiftly away. The three assassins were undoubtedly Jesse and Frank James and Clell Miller, for within an hour after the murder these three met a gentleman upon the highway and informed him of Mr. Askew's fate, and told him the murder was in consequence of the acts of Pinkerton's detectives.

This cowardly act, by which a peaceable citizen had been made to surrender up his life for the sake of a savage revenge, destroyed again every spark of sympathy for the desperadoes, and the determination for their capture was renewed. Armed posses of Clay county citizens set out in search of the assassins, but the pursuit was in vain, and after a week of earnest effort, finding no trace of the brigands, the party returned to their homes, each one recking how soon his turn might come to add to the gory record of the remorseless freebooters.

THE SAN ANTONIO STAGE ROBBERY.

AFTER the murder of Mr. Askew, the bandits, in anticipation of renewed efforts to effect their capture, left Missouri and visited their old haunts in the southwest. They spent several days in the Indian Territory for the purpose of learning with what persistency and the character of the search being made by the authorities. Finding that all effort at their apprehension was confined to western Missouri, the outlaws rode into Texas and soon formed a plan for robbing the stage running between San Antonio and Austin. To plan was to execute, and on the 12th of May, 1875, Jesse James, Clell Miller, Jim Reed and Cole and Jim Younger selected a spot on the highway, about twenty-three miles south-west of Austin, and there ambushed themselves to await the coming of the stage.

It was late in the evening, the sun just descending behind the hills and the chirrup of twilight insects had begun to echo in the solitude of the place. Eleven passengers, three of whom were ladies, were cheerily cracking jokes and relieving the discomforts of the journey by agreeable conversation. Suddenly the driver descried five horsemen riding out into the road one hundred yards ahead of the stage and advancing leisurely. Their appearance and conduct looked suspicous, but as no robberies had been perpetrated on the highway for many years, the driver did not realize what the act portended until, as the stage bowled up, the five men, drawing their pistols, commanded a halt. The order being accompanied by such persuasive authority of course the obedience of the driver was prompt. Then the passengers wondered what it meant, but before they could propound a question four of the brigands rode up on either side of the stage and ordered the inmates to get out. The women, seeing such cruel looking men and their fiercer looking pistols, screamed and scrambled over the male passengers with utter disregard of propriety, and created much confusion. Jesse James and Cole Younger did the talking for the bandits, and in courteous language assured the ladies they had nothing to fear provided the passengers acted with discretion. Soon the eleven but recently gay travelers were arranged in single file along the road behind the stage, and as not the slightest resistance was offered Frank James and Jim Younger had no difficulty in expeditiously relieving all the passengers of their money, watches and other valuables. Among the number was John Breckenridge, president of the First National Bank at San Antonio, from whom $1,000 were obtained; Bishop Gregg, of Austin, contributed his gold watch and nearly $50 in money, while from the other passengers sums from $25 to $50 were obtained.

Having completed the personal plunder, the bandits cut open the two mail bags from which a goodly sum of money was secured, but the amount has not been estimated. The haul aggregated, perhaps, $3,000, which they placed in a sack carried for the purpose, and then, bidding the passengers adieu, the border desperadoes rode swiftly into the shadows, leaving the surprised party to resume their journey in a less amiable mood.

THE GREAT TRAIN ROBBERY AT MUNCIE.

NOTHING was heard of the bandits for several months after the stage robbery, and their crimes were again relegated to partially forgotton incidents of the past. In December following, however, another attack by the outlaws refreshed the memory of their deeds and threw Missouri and Kansas into a fever of intense excitement.

The band of desperadoes, by some means known only to themselves, learned of an intended large shipment of gold-dust from Denver, via Kansas Pacific Railroad, and that it would be carried by a train arriving in Kansas City on a certain day. The place selected at which to intercept the train bearing the valuable shipment, was Muncie, a little, station six miles west of Wyandotte, Kansas. There was a water tank near the place, at which the engines almost invariably stopped to take a fresh supply of water. At this point six bandits stationed themselves and awaited the train, which was not due until after nightfall. Prompt upon time the engine blew its shrill whistle, and then rolled up under the tank and stopped. In a moment the brigands left their place of concealment and boarded the train, one of them, Bill McDaniels, being deputed to cover and remain with the engineer and fireman. The robbers rushed through the cars and commanded every passenger to remain quiet under penalty of death. Two of them stood on the platforms of the cars while the other three proceeded to the express car. The bandits presented their pistols at the head of the messenger and forced him to open the safe, from which the sum of $25,000 in money was taken and gold-dust valued at $30,000. This total sum secured was so large that no attempt was made to rob any of the passengers, and after the valuable plunder was placed in a sack, Jesse James blew a keen whistle and a moment after all the free-booters abandoned the train and regained their horses.

Soon as the passengers reached Wyandotte, which was speedily, the alarm was given, which spread to Kansas City, and another large body of men was sent in pursuit of the daring highwaymen. They chased the fugitives southward into Indian Territory, but the pursuit was abandoned in the Creek Nation, where all traces were blotted out.

About one month after this great robbery a police officer arrested Bill McDaniels in Kansas City, for drunkenness, his participation in the train plundering not then being suspected. But when searched at the police station a sheep-skin bag was found on his person filled with gold-dust. In addition to this he had a large roll of money, and being known in Kansas City as a worthless fellow, suspicion was at once excited that he was a confederate of the train robbers. He was placed in the calaboose and allowed to sober up, and then taken upon a requisition to Lawrence, Kansas. On the following day after his arrest the city marshal and Con O'Hara, the detective, went into McDaniels' cell and spent two hours in a persistent endeavor to obtain a confession from him of his complicity in the robbery, or the names of those who committed the act. But he remained as silent as if he had lost the power of speech, and not a word concerning the robbery did the officers ever hear from him. Two months after his apprehension, in taking him from the jail for trial, McDaniels broke from the deputy sheriff and escaped. After a week's search he was found, but resisting arrest, he was mortally wounded by a member of a citizens' posse named Bauermann. McDaniels died, however, refusing to reveal anything in regard to his confederates. It has since been ascertained, however, that those engaged in the Muncie robbery consisted of Jesse James, Arthur McCoy, Cole and Bob Younger, Clell Miller and McDaniels, the latter only being captured.

THE HUNTINGTON BANK ROBBERY.

AFTER the train robbery the highwaymen separated, some going to Texas and others to Kentucky. In April, 1876, Frank James, Cole Younger, Tom McDaniels, a brother of Bill, and a small black-eyed fellow called Jack Keen, alias Tom Webb, confederated together for the purpose of perpetrating another bank robbery. Keen had been raised in the eastern part of Kentucky and was well acquainted with the mountainous regions of West Virginia and his native State. It was decided to attack and plunder the bank in Huntington, a town of 2,500 people, on the Ohio river, in West Virginia.

About the 1st of September the four bandits rode into the town under the leadership of Frank James and proceeded directly to the bank, which they reached at 2 P. M. Frank James and McDaniels dismounted, leaving Younger and Keen standing guard on the outside. When Frank and McDaniels entered the bank they found only R. T. Oney, the cashier, and a citizen who was making a deposit; these the robbers covered with their pistols and compelled the cashier to open the safe and deliver up all the money in the bank, amounting to $10,000. Having secured the booty the four outlaws rode rapidly out of town, not a single person in the place having the least suspicion of what had occurred until Mr. Oney spread the news.

A posse of twenty-five citizens, headed by the sheriff, set out in pursuit of the bandits at three o'clock, one hour after the robbery was consummated, and followed the trail with the greatest persistency. The officers in other counties were notified by telegraph, and armed bodies of men were sent out from a dozen towns. One hundred miles south-west of Huntington the robbers were sighted and in an exchange of shots McDaniels was killed. This encouraged the pursuing party, who pressed the bandits so hard that they were forced to abandon their horses and take to the mountain fastnesses of Kentucky. The pursuit continued unabated for four weeks, and at length the outlaws were driven out of Kentucky and into Tennessee; here Keen was captured and taken back to Huntington, where he made a confession and was sentenced to eight years imprisonment in the penitentiary. Frank James and Cole Younger eluded pursuit and returned to the Indian Territory, where they met Jesse James and his band of highwaymen, and forthwith new plans were laid for another big robbery.

THE ROCKY CUT TRAIN ROBBERY.

SEVEN months elapsed after the Muncie robbery before the desperate brigands, under the leadership of Jesse James, made another attempt to increase their ill-gotten gains. But in the meantime the band of highwaymen was increasing and organizing for another bold stroke. Many outlaws who had found safety in the Indian Nation were anxious to attach themselves to the James and Younger brothers, but very few were received. The noted bandits were excellent judges of human nature, and they were exceedingly careful not to repose confidence in any one who did not possess indisputable evidence of cunning and bravery; men who, in the event of capture, would not betray their comrades at any sacrifice. In July, 1876, arrangements were completed for rifling another treasure-laden train and the Missouri Pacific Railroad was chosen as the line for their operations. The reorganized party of highwaymen, consisting of Jesse and Frank James, Cole, Bob and Jim Younger, Clell Miller, Hobbs Kerry, Charlie Pitts and Bill Chadwell, nine in number, left their rendezvous in the Indian Territory and, riding separately, reached Otterville, Missouri, by a preconcerted understanding, on the 7th of July.

The capture and confession of Hobbs Kerry enables the giving of a minute narrative of all the circumstances connected with the robbery about to be related.

About one mile east of Otterville, a small station in Pittis county, is a place called Rocky Cut, which is a deep stone cleft, from which the train emerges only to strike the bridge across Otter creek. On the south side of the cut is a heavy wood, and in this the robbers concealed themselves to await the train which was not due there until nearly midnight. A watchman was stationed at the bridge, whom Charlie Pitts and Bob Younger arrested and, after taking his signal lantern and placing it in the track at the bridge approach, they securely tied the helpless fellow and then joined the main party. Hobbs Kerry and Bill Chadwell were detailed to watch the horses and keep them prepared for sudden flight.

As the train came dashing through the cut the engineer saw the danger signal and at once concluded something was wrong with the bridge, and he lost no time in having the brakes set and the enjine reversed. The train came to a stop directly in the cut, and as it slowed up seven of the dare-devils leaped upon the cars and with one at each door, the robbers had no trouble in so intimidating the passengers as to prevent attack. Jesse James, the boldest of the bold, was the first to enter the express car, followed by Cole Younger. At the mouth of two heavy navy pistols the messenger was forced to open the safe, which contained fifteen thousand dollars in bank notes. This money was hastily thrown into a sack, and the shrill whistle was given by Jesse, which was the signal for the bandits to leave the train and mount. No effort was made to rob or harm any of the passengers, the single purpose of the bandits, agreed upon before the attack, was to secure only the valuables of the express.

When the train reached Tipton, report of the robbery was telegraphed to every station along the line, and also to St. Louis and Kansas City, and from these points all over the country.

Hobbs Kerry's statement is, that after the perpetration of the crime, the bandits rode southward together very rapidly until nearly daylight, when they entered a deep wood and there divided the money, after which the band rode off in pairs, except the James Boys and Cole Younger, who kept together. Kerry soon separated from Chadwell, who was his companion, and went to Fort Scott, and from there to Parsons, Kansas, thence to Joplin and then to Granby, where he remained for nearly a week, spending a great deal of money in gambling dens, and in his drunken moments let drop such remarks as led to the suspicion that he was a member of the gang that robbed the train. He next made a trip into Indian Territory, but after a short stay in that country he returned to Granby; there he was arrested in the latter part of August. The authorities had no difficulty in obtaining from Kerry the full particulars of the robbery and the names of his confederates. Detectives from all parts of the country, stimulated by the large rewards offered by the express company and Governor Hardin, set out in search of the bandits. Every State was penetrated, every suspicious character put under surveillance, and all the ingenuity that could be devised by experienced hunters of criminals was exercised.

HOBBS KERRY WATCHED BY A DETECTIVE IN A GAMBLING DEN.

The James and Younger boys and Clell Miller, finding the pursuit at an end, returned from the Nation, whither they had first fled, and by stealthy night marches succeeded in reaching Jackson county, where they retired to the robbers' cave and were there safe from pursuit.

THE FATAL ATTACK ON A MINNESOTA BANK.

The efforts of the detectives to capture the outlaws seemed to be chiefly confined to the southwestern States, and learning this the bandits, after remaining within the seclusion of their undiscoverable haunts for a few weeks, grew tired of the inactivity such life imposed, and as Bill Chadwell was well acquainted in Minnesota, it was decided to send Bob Younger out to find him, and through him to perfect a plan for raiding one of the banks in that State. The means of communication between the bandits was such that Chadwell was soon found and brought into conference with the other members.

The purpose of going into Minnesota could not have been merely because of a supposition that a more ample booty might be secured in that State, for there were many richer banks much nearer.

One of the prime motives of the outlaws was undoubtedly to make a stroke in the far north which would confuse the officers in pursuit of them, and thereby draw the attention of the detectives away from the favorite haunts. Aside from this, no sufficient reason for the strange determination of the brigands is assignable.

A decision was soon reached, and it was decided to make an examination of the country, and raid the bank which gave promise of the largest reward with the least chances of surprise or capture. Cole Younger and Chadwell were accordingly despatched as a reconnoitering party, and were to ride three days in advance of the others, take observations and make report by leaving certain pre-arranged signals along the route decided upon. Those engaged in the intended enterprise were the two James Boys, Cole, Jim and Bob Younger, Charlie Pitts, Clell Miller and Bill Chadwell. The expedition started for Minnesota about the 3d of September, 1876, proceeding by railroad directly to Mankato, the place appointed for a meeting with the two bandits sent in advance. A second consultation, held at that place on the 6th of September, resulted in a decision to strike the bank at Northfield, Rice county, a town of 2500 people, on the I. & M. division of the Milwaukee & St. Paul Railroad.

On the afternoon of the 7th the eight desperadoes entered Northfield at a furious pace, discharging their pistols and by direful threats endeavoring to so intimidate the citizens as to prevent resistance.

They rode direct for the bank, which was located fronting the public square, and stopping in front of the institution. Frank and Jesse James and Bob Younger quickly dismounted and entered the bank while the other robbers were left to guard against attack from the outside. J. L. Haywood, the cashier, A. E. Bunker, teller, and Frank Wilcox, bookkeeper, were the only persons in the bank at the time of the entrance of the bandits. Jesse James drew a pistol and presented it at the cashier's head and commanded him to open the safe. Haywood promptly refused, and the next instant he lay dead at the bandit's feet, his brain pierced with a bullet. At this Bunker and Wilcox fled out at the back door, but as they reached the step a bullet from Frank James' pistol plunged through Bunker's shoulder, but it did not impede his flight. The robbers were left alone in the bank, but beyond a small amount lying upon the counter no money could be found, and the bandits, hearing firing in the streets, rushed out just in time to see Bill Chadwell fall from his horse, his heart pierced with a musket ball, and in a few seconds after Clell Miller received a bullet in his breast, and with a groan tumbled mortally wounded to the ground while his horse galloped riderless up the street.

By this time the citizens came rushing to the attack and the firing became general. Jim Younger was shot in the mouth and a horse was wounded.

The effective shots were fired by Dr. Henry Wheeler from a second-story window in the Damphier House, facing the bank. The six unharmed bandits rushed for their horses and rode at their highest speed out of town, followed in fifteen minutes afterward by fifty well mounted citizens. Then succeeded a flight and pursuit which for persistency, endurance, courage and results is without a parallel.

Information of the murder and robbery was telegraphed in every direction and each hour the pursuing force was augmented by volunteers who sprang up in the pathways of the robbers and guarded every highway and bridle path. The chase led through Shieldsville and from there into LeSeur county where, being pressed closely, too Jesse and Frank James insisted on killing Jim Younger, the blood from whose wound was furnishing a trail for the pursuers. This proposition resulted in a separation of the outlaws, Jesse and Frank James remaining together and the Younger boys and Charley Pitts, (whose real name was Sam Wells), remaining in a body. The country was fairly filled with resolute men determined upon the death of the bandits. It was very soon discovered that the robbers had separated and the pursuing parties were divided and put upon the two trails.

About one hundred and fifty miles south-west of Northfield, near a place called Madelia, the Youngers and Charlie Pitts were surrounded in a swamp, and captured after a desperate fight with the citizens' posse Pitts being killed aud all the Youngers receiving fresh wounds. Pitts was buried, and the Youngers, always under guard, after months of suffering finally recovered. After their recovery they pleaded guilty to the charges against them and were sentenced to prison for the term of their natural lives. They are yet in the Minnesota penitentiary at Stillwater. Jesse and Frank James were more fortunate; although so closely pressed that a hundred times they could see and hear the voices of their pursuers, yet they were not discovered. Day and night the James Boys continued their flight, unable to cook anything, subsisting on green corn and raw potatoes; never daring to show their faces, swimming streams, and confining their route to the least accessible sections of country. Extraordinary cunning, a knowledge of men and adaptability to circumstances, after ten days of a most remarkable pursuit, covering their tracks by wading for miles in streams of water, Jesse and Frank James eluded their pursuers and regained their secure haunts in Jackson county.

AT GLENDALE—THE LAST GREAT TRAIN ROBBERY.

THREE years elapsed from the time of the attack at Northfield until the James Boys were heard of again in connection with criminal escapades. Their names existed in tradition, and the horror which was once manifested at the mention of their savage natures had become dwarfed into mere expressions of surprise. It was reported that Frank James had died of consumption in the Indian Nation and that Jesse was living peaceably in one of the remote Territories, following the profitable occupation of cattle-raising.

On the evening of October 7th, 1879, the people of Western Missouri were suddenly shocked by the intelligence of another great train robbery, committed in the old guerrilla haunts, where crime had held such high carnival during the dark period of the great rebellion. On the day in question Jesse James, Jim Cummings, Ed. Miller, a brother of Clell, Daniel (better known as Tucker) Bassham and seven others whose names are not known, appeared suddenly at the little station of Glendale, which is on the line of the Chicago, Alton & St. Louis Railroad, twenty-two miles from Kansas City. The town consists of a post-office and store combined and a station house, and is a flag station only. About six o'clock in the evening the party of bandits rode into the place and proceeded at once to put every one present under arrest, which they readily accomplished, as there were but three men at the station, and these were locked in the station house. The train going east was due at 6:45 P. M., at a time when darkness clothed the scene, and the masked robbers compelled the station operator to display his signal to stop the train. Previous to this preliminary the masked bandits had piled a large number of condemned ties on the track only a few hundred yards east of Glendale, and had everything fully prepared to execute their purpose expeditiously. The train was on time, and seeing the stop signal displayed, the engineer obeyed its import, and in a moment the conductor, John Greenman, was facing an ominous pistol, while others of the robbers covered the engineer and demanded submission. Meeting with no resistance the bandits broke in the door of the express car, but in their efforts to break in the door, William Grimes, the messenger, hastily unlocked the safe and took out thirty-five thousand dollars in money and valuables, which he attempted to conceal. He was too late, however, for at the moment he was placing the money bag behind some boxes in the car, the door yielded and three robbers rushed on him. Refusing to deliver the safe-key, Grimes was knocked down and badly punished. The key was taken from him and the few remaining contents of value in the safe were appropriated, as was also the bag containing the money.

The haul was a very rich one and the attempt having been successful the passengers were not molested, and the train was permitted to depart after a detention of no more than ten minutes.

The commission of this crime again aroused the officers, and as Glendale is in Jackson county, Major

James Leggitt, the county marshal, took immediate steps to discover and arrest the perpetrators. Being a shrewd and fearless man, he went to work intelligently and unceasingly. He soon discovered who composed the party that committed the robbery, notwithstanding the fact that they were heavily masked.

Tucker Bassham, one of the robbers, who was raised in Jackson county, was suspected directly after the deed was accomplished. He left the county for a time, but returned and buried his share of the booty, which was one thousand one hundred dollars. Soon he began to exhibit an unusual amount of money, and a spy was placed upon him until enough information was obtained to conclusively establish his connection with the robbery. But Marshal Leggitt deferred the arrest with the hope that he might learn of some communication between Bassham and other members of the gang, and accomplish their arrest. In June last (1880) deputy marshals W. G. Keshler and M. M. Langhorn, arrested Bassham and lodged him in the jail at Kansas City. Shortly afterward Major Leggitt obtained a full confession from his prisoner, which was reduced to writing and made in the form of an affidavit.

SHOOTING OF JESSE JAMES BY GEO. SHEPHERD.

THE pursuit of the Glendale robbers did not cease after a week's efforts, as previously, but Maj. Leggitt was determined to accomplish his purpose. He resolved upon an expedient which evidences his cunning and strategy: Living in Kansas City, at the time of the robbery, was George Shepherd, one of the most courageous men that ever faced danger. He was one of Quantrell's lieutenants and fought in all the terrible and unmerciful encounters of that chief of the black banner. He was at Lawrence, and rode beside the James Boys in that dreadful cyclone of remorseless murder. He had run the gauntlet of a hundred rifles and fought against odds which it appeared impossible to escape. After the close of the war Jesse James accepted Geo. Shepherd as a leader and followed him into Texas, and would still be following his counsels had not circumstances separated them.

Maj. Leggitt evolved a scheme out of his hours of study looking towards the capture of Jesse James. He sent for Shepherd, who was working for Jesse Noland, a leading dry goods merchant of Kansas City, and to the ex-guerrilla he proposed his scheme. It was this: Shepherd, being known to have formerly been a comrade of Jesse James, it was to be reported that undoubted information had reached the authorities establishing Shepherd's connection with the Glendale robbery. A report of this was to be printed upon a slip of paper having printed matter upon the reverse side, so as to appear like a newspaper clipping. Shepherd was to take this printed slip, find Jesse James and propose to join him, saying that he was being hounded by detectives, and, although innocent, he felt that his only safety was in uniting his fortunes with Jesse and his fearless band. This being accomplished, Shepherd was to find an opportunity for killing Jesse James, and the reward for him, dead or alive, was to be divided. In addition to this, Shepherd was to be provided with a horse and to receive $50 per month during the time of his service.

The conditions and terms were satisfactory to Shepherd, and in the latter part of October, about two weeks after the Glendale robbery, he started out in quest of Jesse James.

The plan of Shepherd's operations and the manner in which he accomplished his hazardous undertaking is herewith detailed just as he related the story to the writer, and other corroborative testimony establishes its truth:

When Shepherd left Kansas City he was mounted upon a sorrel horse and his weapons consisted of a thirty-two calibre single-barrel pistol and a small pocket-knife. He rode directly to the Samuels residence, which he reached at dusk, and tied his horse in a thicket about two hundred yards from the house. He found Mrs. Samuels and the Doctor at home just preparing to sit down to supper. The story that any enmity existed on the part of Jesse James against Shepherd is untrue; reports of this kind may have been circulated but there was not a semblance of truth in them. Shepherd was warmly received by Mrs. Samuels and her husband, and at their invitation he took supper with them. While they were eating, Shepherd explained that his life and liberty were in great jeopardy and that owing to reports, false as they were, of his connection with the Glendale robbery, he had been forced to flee, and for mutual protection he wished to join Jesse James and his confederates; thereupon Shepherd produced the apparently newspaper clipping already referred to, which Dr. and Mrs. Samuels both read. After finishing supper Dr. Samuels told Shepherd to ride to a certain point in the main highway where he would meet Jesse and some of his associates. The Dr. went out into the woods where he knew the bandits were concealed, while Shepherd mounted his horse and rode to the spot indicated, where, after waiting for less than five minutes, he was met by Jesse James, Jim Cummings, Ed. Miller and another party whom Shepherd did not know. Shepherd repeated his story to Jesse James and showed him the clipping, after which he was immediately received into the full confidence of Jesse and the band. Why should Jesse have entertained suspicions? Shepherd had been his intimate comrade for many years; the two had ridden and fought together in a hundred terrible conflicts, and were associated together in the Kentucky bank robbery. Shepherd was the very man of all others whom Jesse wanted for a companion in his daring deeds and it was unnatural, under the circumstances, for any of the bandits to doubt Shepherd's story.

The party remained all night at the Samuels residence and on the following day they proceeded to a spot in Jackson county called "Six Mile," which is eighteen miles from Kansas City, and spent the day at Benjamin Marr's. It was here a plan was laid for robbing the bank at Empire City, in Jasper county. After the scheme was fully understood Shepherd told Jesse that it would be necessary for him to procure a better horse and some effective weapons, which he could do at a friend's near Kansas City. Jesse urged Shepherd then to return at night to the friend's place, get a good horse and at least two heavy pistols and meet the party at Six Mile on the third night following.

Shepherd then rode back to Kansas City and imparted the information of his meeting and arrangements with Jesse James to Maj. Leggitt, who provided Shepherd with a splendid horse and three large-sized Smith & Wesson pistols. But in order to prevent any possibility of deception, Maj. Leggitt took Shepherd to Independence and placed him in jail, and then sent three trusted men to Six Mile for the purpose of ascertaining if Jesse James and his party were really rendezvoused at that point. Maj. Leggitt soon learned that Shepherd had reported nothing but facts and he was then sent out, splendidly armed and mounted, for the meeting place. Shepherd did not reach the trysting spot until the morning after the time agreed upon, and he found Jesse and his followers gone, but the party at whose house the meeting was to occur—Benj. Marr's—gave Shepherd the following letter, which is herewith copied verbatim.

Friend Georg.

I cant wate for you hear, I want you to meet me on Rogs Iland, and we will talk about that Business we spok of. I would wate for you but the boys wants to leave hear, dont fale to come and if we dont by them cattle I will come back with you. Come to the plase whear we meet going south that time and stay in that naborhood untill I find you.

Your Friend.

J—— ——

Thus instructed Shepherd started for Rogue's Island, but met Jesse James at the head of Grand River. This fact furnishes one of the proofs of Jesse's anxiety to have Shepherd as a comrade, for he was so anxious lest Shepherd would not meet them, or fail to get the letter he left with Marr, that he returned to find him. Jesse and Shepherd returned to the camp, where they found Cummings, Miller and the unknown, and then the party rode directly for Empire City, the vicinity of which they reached about noon on Saturday, November 1, 1879. They went into camp on Short Creek, eight miles south of Empire City, and at four o'clock in the afternoon it was agreed that Shepherd should ride into the town and learn what he could respecting the surroundings and location of the bank. It was after dark when Shepherd reached the place, and, pursuing his story, he was astonished at finding the bank lighted up and a close inspection revealed to him a dozen men inside the bank armed with double-barreled shot-guns. Shepherd stated to the writer that Maj. Leggitt must have notified the bank officers of the intended raid, by telegraph, but Maj. Leggitt denies having done so, and says that Shepherd must have told some person who communicated with the bank. Anyhow the arrangement was that Maj. Leggitt was to be in Empire City with a good force of assistants and was to be aided by Shepherd in capturing the outlaws when the attack on the bank should be made. Circumstances prevented Maj. Leggitt from appearing in Empire City at the time agreed upon, but he sent word to the town authorities.

Finding everything in readiness to meet the intended attack, Shepherd went into a restaurant and while eating his supper, Tom Cleary, an old acquaintance, came in and greeted him. After supper the two went to Cleary's house and remained all night, and Shepherd told his friend the part he was acting in the effort to capture Jesse James. Ed. Cleary, a brother of Tom's, was also informed of the scheme and Shepherd asked their assistance, or to at least follow him the next morning to the camp of the bandits. The understanding was at the time Shepherd left the outlaws that he should return to the camp by nine o'clock Sunday morning and, if his report was favorable, the raid on the bank would be made Sunday night.

Shepherd kept the appointment and returned to the place where the bandits had encamped, but found the camp deserted. He thought this strange, but soon found the old sign of a "turn-out" had been made to let him know where they were. It is well known that the James Boys and their comrades frequently separate. They have a sign, however, by which it is not difficult for them to find one another. This sign is the crossing of two twigs along the highway, which indicates that one or more of the parties, according to the number of twigs, has turned out of the highway at that point. Shepherd saw the twigs and after riding about half a mile in the direction the branches lay he found the party, all of whom were slightly intoxicated. He knew they had no whiskey with them when he left on Saturday afternoon, and at once concluded they had been in town. Cummings was the first to speak. Said he:

Shooting of Jesse James.

"The bank is guarded; how is this?" Shepherd responded: "Yes, and I think the best thing for us to do is to separate and get out of this."

Cummings had ridden into Galena on Saturday night, where he had purchased some whiskey and there heard rumors of the intended bank raid.

The party agreed with Shepherd that it would be wise for them to get out of that section, and they mounted their horses and divided, riding southward. Ed. Miller's position was one hundred yards to the right while Cummings and the unknown rode at the same distance to the left of the center which was taken by Jesse James and Shepherd. The woods were open enough for all parties to remain in sight of each other.

When they reached a point twelve miles south of Galena, all parties maintaining their respective positions, Shepherd gave a smart jerk to the bridle rein which caused his horse to stop while Jesse rode on. It was the work of an instant, for as Jesse's horse gained two steps forward Shepherd drew one of his large pistols and without speaking a word fired, the ball taking effect in Jesse's head one inch behind the left ear. Only the one shot was fired, for Shepherd saw the result of the shot, and Jesse plunged headlong from his horse and lay motionless on the ground as if death had been instantaneous. Shepherd says he viewed the body for nearly one minute before either of the other outlaws made any demonstration.

Ed. Miller first started toward him in a walking pace, and then Cummings, and the unknown drew their pistols and rode swiftly after him. Shepherd's horse was swift and he put him to the greatest speed, soon distancing the unknown, but Cummings was mounted on a superior animal and the chase for three miles was a hot one. Each of the two kept firing, but the rapid rate at which they were riding made the shots ineffectual. Seeing that he was pursued only by Cummings who was gaining on him, Shepherd stopped and wheeled his horse and at that moment a bullet struck him in the left leg just below the knee, producing, however, only a flesh wound. As Cummings dashed up Shepherd took deliberate aim and fired, and Cummings reeled in the saddle, turned his horse and retreated. Shepherd says he feels confident that he struck Cummings hard in the side, and that he killed Jesse James. He rode back to Galena where he remained two weeks under a surgeon's care, and after recovery returned to Kansas City.

That Shepherd told the truth there is no room for doubt, and he had the best reasons for believing that he had killed Jesse James; but two parties, at least, whose word is reliable affirm that they have seen Jesse James since the shooting and that Cummings has also been met by them, who stated that Shepherd did shoot Jesse, and that the bullet did strike him just behind the left ear, but instead of penetrating the brain it had coursed around the skull partially paralyzing the brain and spine. Cummings further stated that while Jesse James was still living his career as a bandit was ended forever by the bullet from Shepherd's pistol. In other words, Jesse's mind has been totally destroyed. How much truth there is in this report is left for conjecture. Mrs. Samuels says she believes that Jesse is dead, and a meeting which she had with Shepherd since the shooting was such as caused those who witnessed it, to believe the woman was earnest in that opinion.

WHY DID SHEPHERD SHOOT JESSE JAMES?

THE prime motive which actuated George Shepherd in shooting Jesse James has never been suspicioned by more than one man, and acting upon suggestions made by that single person, the writer verified the theory. It is true that the rewards, amounting to nearly one hundred thousand dollars, for the apprehension or dead body of Jesse James, were a strong temptation, and it certainly had its influence with Shepherd, but there was a stronger motive.

Directly after the war Ike Flannery, a nephew of George Shepherd, reached the age of manhood and came into possession of five thousand dollars, a sum he had inherited from the estate of his deceased father. Ike was somewhat wayward and was well acquainted with the James Boys and the guerrillas. Jesse James and Jim Anderson, a brother of the notorious Bill, knew of Ike Flannery's inheritance, and they induced him to buckle on his pistols, take his money and go with them upon a pretended expedition. Near Glasgow, Missouri, the three stopped at the house of a friend where there were three girls, the men of the house being away on business. After eating dinner the three started away, but they had been gone only a few moments when the report of two pistol shots was heard and Jim Anderson came riding back to the house where they had dined, and told the girls that his party had been fired on by the militia, and that Flannery had been killed. Jesse James and Anderson rode away while the girls notified some of the neighbors, and when the body of Flannery was found in the road, there were two bullet holes in the head and the five thousand dollars were missing. Shepherd did not learn all the circumstances connected with Flannery's death until sometime afterward, but when he was told how Anderson and Jesse James acted, he was convinced that they murdered his nephew and plundered his dead body.

It was more than one year after this tragic occurrence before Shepherd met either of the murderers. He was in Sherman, Texas, when Jim Anderson came up to him with a cordial greeting, little suspecting the terrible result of that meeting. The two drank together and appeared on the best of terms until the hour of eleven o'clock at night. The saloon was closing and the darkness without was most uninviting. Shepherd asked Anderson to accompany him over to the court-house yard as he wanted to talk secretly concerning a certain transaction.

When the two reached the yard, and about them was nothing but sombre shadow and the quiet of sleep, cautiously, yet determinedly, Shepherd drew from its sheath a long, bright, deadly knife, which gathered on its blade and focused the light unseen before, and then made ready for a horrible deed. Anderson had never thought of danger until the keen edge of the terrible weapon was at his throat.

Said Shepherd: "You murdered Ike Flannery and robbed his body of five thousand dollars. I have determined to avenge his death, and to accomplish my purpose I brought you here. What have you got to say?"

Anderson had killed many men and he knew how to die. There was no begging, no denying, only a realization of what he could not avert; and he accepted fate with a stoicism worthy of a religious fanatic. Before receiving the fatal stroke, however, he told Shepherd that Jesse James was the one who proposed the murder and robbery of young Flannery, and that each fired a fatal shot and then divided the stolen money. When this admission escaped his lips, Shepherd sprang upon him like a tiger, drew the glittering blade of the terrible knife across his throat, and the spirit of the murderer and robber took its flight into the realms of the unknown.

On the following morning a dead body with a ghastly gash in the throat, from which the blood had poured until it dyed the grass a yard in diameter, was found and identified as that of Jim Anderson. DeHart, an old-time guerrilla, was in Sherman at the time of the murder, and was known to have a grudge against the murdered man, so suspicion attached to him so strongly that he had to leave Texas. No one ever suspected Shepherd of the murder, but his own confessions to the writer are given in this account of Anderson's execution.

Shepherd has longed for an opportunity to kill Jesse James, but the surroundings, even during a long association, were never sufficiently favorable. The opportunity was exceedingly unfavorable at Short Creek, but revenge and the promise of such an immense reward nerved him to the undertaking.

ROBBERY OF THE MAMMOTH CAVE STAGES.

The James Boys, and especially Frank, nave remained in seclusion for a considerable period, and

Settling an Old Score.

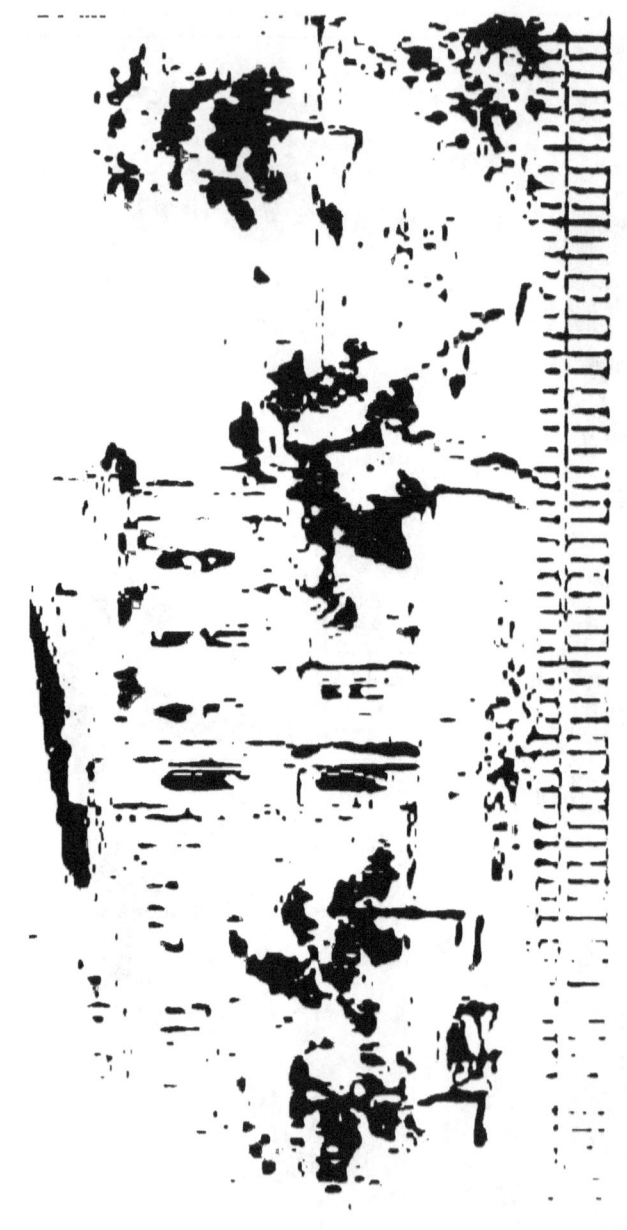

with the shooting of Jesse—whom many still believe to be dead—it was thought that the old remnants of guerrilla plunderers had entirely disappeared. It is positively known that Frank James resided in Baltimore during the winter of 1879-80, and his home was located on one of the principal resident streets. At that time he wore full whiskers which were very long, reaching to his waist. The name he bore while in Baltimore the writer has not been able to learn, for obvious reasons. He disappeared from that city in March last, and it is reported by Kansas City police officers that Frank was seen in Jackson county, Missouri, by two of his acquaintances in the latter part of July, 1880, and that his whiskers were cut short. The following account of the robbery of the Mammoth Cave stage again brings Frank James and Jim Cummings prominently into notice.

The Concord stage running between Mammoth Cave and Cave City, in Edmonson county, Kentucky, was captured by highwaymen on the afternoon of Friday, September 3d, 1880, and the passengers despoiled of everything they carried.

At this season of the year Mammoth Cave is visited by thousands of tourists and sight-seers, who are usually people of means, furnishing fat pickings for the robbers. One of the routes to the cave, and the one selected by the large majority of its visitors, is by way of the Louisville and Nashville Railroad to Cave City, and thence by the Concord stages to the cave, which is about eight or ten miles distant. The stage road is through a lonely and rocky region, and about midway on the route it runs through a dense wood, which adds considerably to its dreariness. About 6 o'clock Friday evening, while the coach from the cave was coming to Cave City, it reached this wood, and while coming through the narrow road in a walk, two men, one mounted on a thin black thoroughbred horse, and the other on a fine sorrel, rode out of the dense forest, and, dashing up to the stage, covered the driver and passengers with their revolvers and called a halt. The stage was pulled up, the driver was ordered down and to the door of his vehicle, and then calmly dismounting and holding their horses by the bridle reins, the work of delivering the booty began. The rider of the black horse, a man about thirty-five years old, with a straggling red mustache and beard, was the leader and spokesman. He was rather small, not appearing to be over five feet six inches in height, and would weigh about 140 pounds. He had light blue eyes, a pleasant smile and distributed his attentions to the defenseless party of eight passengers with a sang froid and easy politeness which did much to alleviate their feelings. His accomplice was about the same age, with black whiskers and mustache rather ragged in trim, and had a pair of black eyes. He was rather slow in his movements, but the business in hand suffered nothing for that.

"Come out of the stage, please," said the spokesman, in a light, high pitched voice.

The passengers looked through the open windows and saw the muzzels of the impassive revolvers covering the whole length of the vehicle, and, as there was not a weapon in the party as large as a penknife, they could not resist or parley. There were seven gentlemen and one lady in the coach, and the lady naturally was nervous and alarmed. In the excitement and bustle attendant upon rising and leaving their seats, Mr. R. S. Rountree, of the Milwaukee *Evening Wisconsin*, who was making the trip with relatives, slipped his pocket-book and gold watch under the cushion of the seat.

Very few words were spoken, though the highwaymen seemed impatient and ordered them to "hurry up." As each gentleman stepped out he was covered with the muzzle of a revolver and told to take his place in line and hold up his hands. The lady, a daughter of Hon. R. H. Rountree, of Lebanon, Ky., was permitted to remain in the stage. After the passengers were all out the leader of the two villains tossed his rein to his accomplice, who covered the line while the spokesman proceeded to rifle their pockets, talkingly pleasantly as he went. J. E. Craig, Jr., of Lawrenceville, Ga., lost $670; Hon. R. H. Rountree, of Lebanon, Ky., handed out a handsome gold watch, valued at $200, and $55 in cash; S. W. Shelton, of Calhoun, Tenn., gave up about $50; Miss

Lizzie Rountree, of Lebanan, Ky., lost nothing but rings, one of them a handsome diamond; S. H. Frohlichstein, of Mobile, Ala., lost $23; Geo. M. Paisley, of Pittsburg, gave up $33; W. G. Welsh, of Pittsburg, lost $5 and a handsome watch. R. S. Rountree, of Milwaukee, saved his money as stated. Hon. R. H. Rountree felt very sore over the loss of an elegant engraved watch, which was presented by Hon. J. Proctor Knott, the member of Congress from the Fourth District.

The spokesman of the marauders explained that they were not highwaymen, but moonshiners, and were pursued so hotly by the government officers that they were compelled to have money to get out of the country. He asked each passenger his name and place of residence, and noted them down, saying that some day he would repay them their losses When he came to Mr. Craig, of Georgia, he remarked that he hated to take his money because he had fought in a Georgia regiment during the war, but the case was a desperate one and he was compelled to do it.

When Miss Rountree gave her name and place of residence at Lebanon, a pleased smile lighted up the robber's face, and he asked:

"Do you know the Misses —— of Lebanon?"

"Quite well," answered the young lady.

"So do I," he rejoined, "and they are nice girls. Give them my regards when you see them, and tell them I will make this right some day."

After getting all the valuables of the party the marauders returned the pocket-books with the railway passes and tickets, and giving the passengers orders to get in, mounted and rode off. They told the passengers, for consolation, that they had robbed the out stage, getting $700 from Mr. George Croghan, one of the owners of the cave.

The rider of the black horse was Frank James, and his companion was Jim Cummings. These facts have been fully established by information of an indisputable character, which came into the possession of the writer since the robbery.

PERSONAL CHARACTERISTICS OF THE JAMES BOYS.

SINGULAR as it may appear, there is scarcely a single feature of similarity in the character of the James brothers. Frank James is a man of more than ordinary education, and his manners show some effort at refinement. He is very slim, and not more than five feet six inches in height, and weighs about one hundred and forty pounds. He has blue eyes, very light hair and usually wears a shortly cropped full beard and straggling mustache, of a pale, reddish color. His face is peculiar in shape, being broad at the forehead and tapering abruptly from the cheek bones to the chin, which is almost pointed. In his motions he is neither naturally slow nor quick, but at times he affects either. His cunning and coolness are remarkable, and to compare the two boys in this respect would be like comparing the boldest highwayman with the lowest sneak thief, so great is Frank's superiority. In the matter of education Frank has improved his opportunities and is a student, being a lover of books and familiar with the different phases of life. He has murdered many men, and yet he is not destitute of mercy, and finds no gratification in deeds of blood. He has tried to imitate the traditions of Claude Duval, whose fictitious adventures Frank has read until he can repeat them like the written narrative.

Jesse James is a strongly made man, standing five feet ten inches in height, and will weigh one hundred and sixty-five pounds. He has brown eyes, dark hair and is of a nervous temperament. Jesse's peculiarity is in his eyes which are never at rest. In his youth Jesse was troubled with granulated eyelids from which he has never fully recovered, which is seen in the constant batting of his eyes and a slight irritation of the lids; besides this marked peculiarity, the first joint of the forefinger on his left hand is missing. He usually wears full whiskers of apparently one month's growth. His education is very limited, barely enabling him to read and write. He is revengeful in his nature, always sanguine, impetuous, almost heedless. It is due to Frank James' strategy and Jesse's desperate bravery that the latter has not long since been punished for his crimes. In deeds of violence Jesse finds especial delight, and in his entire nature there is not a trace of mercy.

It is asserted, by those who know them best, that Jesse and Frank are only half-brothers, having the same mother, but that Jesse's father is a physician in Clay county. What truth there is in this report the writer does not assume the responsibility of confirming, giving it only as the assertion of many prominent men of Clay county.

On one occasion, so George Shepherd relates, while Jesse and Frank were dining with their mother, with Shepherd as their guest, a dispute arose over a trivial matter, in which the brothers became very angry and drew their pistols. Mrs. Samuels made no effort to interfere, and the difficulty terminated without a fight. In the row Frank told Jesse that he knew they were not brothers, to which assertion neither Jesse nor Mrs. Samuels made any reply.

It is well known among the confederates of the James Boys, and it has been so declared by Shepherd, the Younger boys and Cummings, that there was no love between Frank and Jesse, and Shepherd told the writer that instead of Frank avenging the attack on Jesse at Short Creek he would applaud it. Going still farther, Shepherd said that at his last meeting with Frank, two years ago, the latter declared he would kill Jesse if he ever met him again; that Jess, as he called him, had tried to have him (Frank) ambushed and captured in Texas, and that that was not the first time Jess had played the stake to have him murdered.

The fact of Jim Cummings' association with Frank James in the robbery of the Mammoth Cave stage coaches gives color of truth to Shepherd's declaration that he killed Jesse James near Galena, or to Cummings' statement that Shepherd's shot, while not killing Jesse, had paralyzed his brain and destroyed his mind.

Frank James was married to Miss Annie Ralston, of Jackson county, in September, 1875. The marriage was one of those romantic episodes which brought great sorrow to Mr. Ralston, an industrious farmer living eight miles from Kansas City. Miss Annie was but a school girl whose reading of dime novels had so far impaired her judgment as to make her long for the association of a hero. Her meeting with Frank James was accidental, but she had read of his exploits and he was her ideal. Annie left her home clandestinely and met Frank James many miles from the old homestead; a Baptist minister performed the ceremony and the outlaw and his now ostracised wife went into the shadows of cave and forest, severing the bonds which bound them to society and civilization.

When Mr. Ralston learned of the desperate step taken by his daughter he was almost crazed with grief. He went direct to Kansas City and, with eyes suffused with tears, begged Judge Mumford, of the *Times*, to prepare for him and publish an article which would relieve him of the stigma which might attach to him by the error of his daughter. Mr. Ralston was anxious the public should know that he never had any association with the outlaw and that,

'FRANK JAMES WINS A BRIDE.

though Annie had been a child who had filled his heart with love, yet her alliance with a highwayman had banished the very memory of her from the fond heart which would know her no more. Such an article did appear in the *Times*, and if Mr. Ralston ever became reconciled to his bandit son-in-law his neighbors never learned the fact.

Jesse James was married to his cousin, Miss Zerelda Mimms, in the Autumn of 1874, at the home of his mother in Clay county. Miss Mimms was an orphan, who had lived with a married sister in Kansas City. Being of age there was no one to criticise her act, and she stepped across the threshold of prescribed citizenship to share the perils of an outlaw's life.

The peculiar profession followed by Jesse and Frank James has prevented them from having any permanent residence, and their wives have been compelled, in a measure, to lead a life of seclusion, traveling from place to place, concealing their identity and experiencing few pleasures because of the constant anxiety to which they are subjected. It is understood that Frank is the father of two children, and Jesse finds consolation in two little boys and a baby girl. The outlaw brothers make affectionate husbands and loving and indulgent fathers.

THE UNION PACIFIC EXPRESS ROBBERY.

THE following account of the Union Pacific train robbery is not published in chronological order with other robberies, because it is not certainly known that the James Boys had any connection with it, and in this history of these noted desperadoes we have endeavored to give only such facts as are sustained by indisputable evidence. It is generally believed, however, that the two noted brothers led the party, and, with their usual shrewdness, succeeded in escaping southward with a large amount of booty. The following letter, written by Jesse James to a former comrade, in March previous to the robbery, is strong presumptive evidence that he and Frank were the planners and executors of the scheme, and that they had it in contemplation even before the raid into Minnesota:

FORT WORTH, March 10th, '77.

DEAR ———

The boys will soon be ready. As soon as the roads dries up, and the streams runs down, we will drive. We expect to take in a good bunch of cattle. You may look out. There will be lots of bellering after the drive. Remember it's business. The rainge is good, I learn, between Sidney and Dedwood. We may go to pasture somewheres in that region. You will hear of it. Tell Sam to come to Honey Grove, Texas, before the drive seson comes. There's money in the stock. As ever,

Jesse J.

There is a mystery connected with the Union Pacific Railroad robbery which, for more than three years, has remained impenetrable and will, doubtless, continue so to the end of time. The particulars of this daring outrage, gathered principally from newspaper reports at the time, are as follows:

On the 10th day of September, 1877, a party of

nine men, well armed and mounted, rode to a point on the Union Pacific R. R. near Ogallala, the capital of Keith county, in the extreme western part of Nebraska. They made no special effort to deceive the people of the town, as the purpose of their visit was never mentioned. On the day following the encampment, one of the party, afterwards known to be Jim Berry, a former resident of the State, went into Ogallala and purchased four large red handkerchiefs and a gallon of whiskey. That night the camp presented a hilarious scene and the wild orgies were continued such an unusually long time that the citizens began to make remarks respecting the character of the nine strange men. Three days afterward the camp was abandoned, none of the citizens knowing which direction the party had taken, so that suspicion was directed against the object of the singular visitors.

On the 18th following, the mysterious nine suddenly appeared at a small station called Big Springs, fifteen miles west of Ogallala, where the engines of the Union Pacific railroad almost invariably stop for water. The express train was due from the west at eight o'clock, P. M., and the party disposed themselves, directly after dark, in favorable positions for the work in hand. Promptly upon time the train came thundering up to the station and the engine stopped under the water tank. As the fireman was about to mount the tender for the purpose of directing

AN ENGINEER WHO MEANT FIGHT.

the water spout, two men wearing red handkerchiefs for masks rushed up toward the engine. For some reason the engineer had a presentiment that some trouble was brewing, so seizing his pistol he stepped to the side of the cab and peered into the darkness. It was too late; the fire through the open furnace door reflected his actions distinctly and in a moment the engineer realized that he was looking down into the fatal depths of four navy revolvers and he and the fireman were forced to surrender and keep quiet.

At the same time the two robbers took possession of the engine, two others, with the same mask of red handkerchiefs, boarded the express car, while the other five commenced discharging their pistols in order to intimidate the passengers. The express messenger made an effort at resistance, but he was struck a desperate blow on the head with a pistol and then forced to deliver up the keys to the Wells, Fargo & Co.'s safe. The contents of the safe in gold, silver and currency amounted to $60,000, besides 300,000 ounces of silver in bars, the latter consigned to the Treasury at Washington. The robbers could not handle the heavy silver bars, so they were compelled to be satisfied with the other contents of the safe and about $2,000 which they took from the passengers. They then permitted the train to go on its way, and having divided their plunder they loaded the coin on three pack-mules and made off with it.

The men had been carelessly masked and a passenger had recognized one of them as a fellow named Joel Collins, who had been passing for a stock man about that section. From this the railroad detectives obtained information on which to act, and though the pursuit which was organized failed to overtake the outlaws, there was still a hope of recovering some of the treasure. Part of the gang had gone directly south into Kansas, and word was sent along the Kansas Pacific to be on the lookout for them. On the 25th of September, Sheriff Bardsley and ten soldiers were patroling a section of the road near Buffalo station. They had a description of one of the parties who were expected to strike about that point, and sure enough two men were seen coming down from the north with a pack animal. The soldiers kept out of sight in a ravine near by, and when the men reached the station and were watering their horses the sheriff talked with them long enough to be satisfied that they were the men he was expecting. They only stopped a few minutes, then pushed on south. The sheriff immediately brought out his squad and demanded a halt, calling Collins by name. The men even then did not seem to apprehend that they were known as the train robbers, but on being told to surrender they drew their pistols. This brought a volly from the cavalrymen which killed them both. In the pack was found $20,000 of the gold. Collins' companion's name was Bass, and he is generally supposed to have been the Texas desperado, Sam Bass. The point at which this treasure was first recovered was only 300 miles south of where the robbery occurred. Subsequently the detectives succeeded in tracing several others of the band and making them give up some of the money, but the greater part of it was lost. It was claimed at the time that Jesse and Frank James were along with this band and that they made enough out of the haul to reimburse themselves very well for what they lost on the Northfield trip.

After the fight at Buffalo the remaining bandits separated for the purpose of dividing the trail which was being followed closely, and the hope was indulged for some time that all the robbers would certainly be apprehended. But after the bandits divided the chase was unavailing and the pursuing parties returned to their homes.

Nearly three weeks after the robbery, Jim Berry returned to Mexico, Missouri, with a large sum of money, principally in gold. He had been a resident of the neighborhood but had left for the Black Hills—so he claimed—some months before. He had never borne a good character and was known to be an acquaintance, at least, of the James and Younger Boys and other noted outlaws. Further than this he was seen in Nebraska, near the place of the robbery, by parties who knew him. The exhibition of so much suddenly acquired wealth, together with the circumstances of the express robbery fresh in the memory of every one, created a suspicion on the part of the sheriff of Audrain county that Berry was one of the robbers. He kept his own counsel, however, and waited further developments. They came soon enough. Berry sold several thousand dollars in gold to the Southern Bank at Mexico; exhibited several fine gold watches which he offered to sell at surprisingly low prices, and besides this he exchanged his ordinary habit for the finest clothes he could have made. Another very suspicious circumstance was in the conduct of Berry; he kept himself in secret places and appeared apprehensive of some effort to catch him. The sheriff, Mr. Glascock, now felt certain that his suspicions were founded upon facts. In the middle of October a young fellow by the name of Bozeman Kazey came into Mexico with an order from Berry for a suit of clothes then being made by a tailor of the place. The sheriff learned of this and he at once arrested Kazey, after which a posse consisting of Robert Steele, John Carter, John Coons and Sam Moore was deputized by the sheriff to assist in the capture of Berry. Kazey was compelled to act as guide, and on the 14th of October the official party set out for the haunts of Berry near Kazey's house. They reached the latter's home before daylight on Sunday morning, and leaving their prisoner in the custody of Steele the remainder of the party surrounded the house for the purpose of catching

Berry when he should come to obtain the clothes he expected Kazey to bring.

Shortly after daylight sheriff Glascock made a little tour out in the woods, and after skirting a bridle path for some distance he saw Berry hitching his horse preparatory to walking to Kazey's house. The sheriff crept cautiously towards Berry and was within forty feet of him before the latter discoverd the officer. Berry then started to run, heedless of the sheriff's cry to halt, and never paused until the second discharge of buckshot from the sheriff's gun tore through his leg and felled him to the ground. Prostrate as he was the bandit tried to draw his pistol, but the sheriff was upon him too quickly. Berry was disarmed and then carried to Kazey's house and surgical aid speedily summoned. On his person was found nearly $1,000 in money, and a fine gold watch and chain.

After the surgeon arrived, Moore, Coons and Steele were left in charge of the wounded man and Kazey, while the sheriff and John Carter rode over to Berry's house to see if new discoveries might not be made.

When they entered the house the sheriff addressed Mrs. Berry and said:

"Mrs. Berry, where is your husband?"

"I am sure I have no idea," she responded; "he has not been at home for several days."

"Then let me inform you," said the sheriff, "that we have just captured him, but in so doing he was badly wounded. You had better go over and see him, at Kazey's house."

Mrs. Berry manifested the greatest grief, and the wailings of the wife and little children quite unnerved the sheriff and his deputy for some time, but they had to do their duty, and, before leaving, the house was thoroughly searched for money and valuables, but nothing was discovered.

On the same afternoon Berry was taken to Mexico in an ambulance and given quarters in the Ringo hotel, where he was attended by the best surgeons in the town. The wound was much more severe than at first supposed. Seven buckshot had penetrated the leg, cutting the arteries and fracturing the tibia bone. His sufferings were excruciating until Monday night when mortification began, and on the following day he died.

At all times Berry positively refused to give the names of his associates in the express robbery, nor did he ever admit his own participation.

The mystery connected with the robbery is found in the impenetrable veil which masks the identity of the robber band. The three who were killed gave no clue as to who were their comrades. In the absence of any proof, judgment being laid entirely upon circumstances and conjecture, it is popularly supposed that the four whose personnel has never been discovered were Sam Bass, Jack Davis and the two James Boys.

AN INTERVIEW WITH THE YOUNGER BROTHERS.

In the early part of September, 1880, Col. George Gaston, of Kansas City, while spending a summer vacation at Minnetonka and the Minnesota lakes, went to Stillwater for the purpose of seeing the Younger Boys, whom he had known before the war. He was accorded an interview with the imprisoned bandits, the result of which was published in the Kansas City *Times* of September 6th, from which the following is taken.

This interview is of special value, considering the obscurity which surrounds the shooting of Jesse James by George Shepherd, and the identity of the James Boys in the Northfield robbery.

After describing his introduction to the prison authorities and entrance into the penitentiary, Mr. Gaston proceeds as follows:

"There was a man at the top of the steps to receive us, another official with the conventional bunch of keys. 'Come this way,' said he, and we followed him into a square room with walls and ceilings of stone. There were chairs and we sat down. A door at one side opened and three men walked in. They were Cole, Jim and Bob Younger. They took chairs opposite and directly facing us. They wore the prison garb, and their faces were shaven and their hair cropped close. They looked so genteel, despite their striped clothing, that my nervousness disappeared at once. I told them who I was and whence I came, and introduced my wife. They were very courteous, and bowed, and said they were glad to see me. Jim hitched back in his chair, and addressing my wife, said, laughingly: 'It is so long since we have been permitted to converse with anybody that I don't know as we can talk.' Then followed a desultory conversation. Cole said his health was poor; he complained of suffering from the effects of the wound in his head, received at the time of his capture. The rifle ball entered near the right ear and lodged under the left ear and has never been removed. Jim was shot in the mouth, but there are now no signs of a wound. Bob had his jaw broken, but he too has entirely recovered, and is the handsomest one in the trio. He is the youngest. I remember him as a boy. He has developed into a robust, fine-looking young man. The escape from death these men had at the time of their capture was a miracle. Sixty guns were discharged at once. Cole and Jim lay on the ground—the one with a bullet through the head and the other with a frightful wound in his mouth; Bob's jaw had been broken but he did not fall—he threw up his arms and cried, 'Don't fire again, gentlemen, they're all dead.' And so they were to all appearance. The pursuers picked them up and carried them back. Slowly they began to mend and ultimately they recovered. By pleading guilty to the crime charged they escaped the death penalty and were sentenced to life imprisonment."

"It was really very touching," pursued Col. Gaston, "to hear them talk of the past and of the present. Cole told of his army life—how at the age of nineteen he had been promoted to a captaincy in the Confederate army. He spoke of the murder of his father and of his career since the close of the war. 'My exploits in the army were exaggerated,' said he, 'just as my exploits as an outlaw have been exaggerated. In one instance I have been too highly praised, and in the other grossly wronged.'

"I learned from their own lips the story of their prison life. Cole Younger is a changed man. I found him positively entertaining. He converses with a correctness, fluency and grace that are charming. None of the brothers are compelled to do very much work; they spend a great deal of their time reading in their cells. Jim is reading law books and Bob is studying medicine; Cole seems to have developed a theological turn of mind. These three men are great favorites in the prison—they are looked up to by their companions as sort of demi-gods, creatures immeasurably above the ordinary inmates of the penitentiary."

"The most dreadful feature of their life," said Col. Gaston, "is the fact that though they occupy adjoining cells, they are not permitted to converse with each other. It is only once a month that they can meet and talk to one another, and then only for a few moments. They told me that they prayed earnestly every night that the month might pass quickly. It was touching beyond expression to hear Cole speak of his early days. His misspent life he charges to the faults of his early training. He says he was taught to be ruled by his passions and his passions alone. And as he talked in this vein the tears came into his eyes and I felt that he was indeed a penitent man. He inquired after his old army friends, and I told him what I knew of them and their whereabouts. In the course of our conversation the James Boys were mentioned. 'Do you believe Jesse is dead?' I asked. Cole straightened up, glanced quick as a lightning flash at his brothers on either side of him, and replied, 'He is, if George Shepherd says he is.' I asked him what he meant, and he answered: 'There are sometimes two things alike in the world, and Jesse James and George Shepherd were as near alike as they could be, in character, I mean. Both are quick, nervous and brave. Jesse was so nervous that sometimes he did things rashly.' As Cole said this he leveled out his right arm as if he were aiming a pistol. Instantaneously it struck me that he sought to convey the impression that it was Jesse James who perpetrated the Northfield bank murder in a moment of nervous rashness. But the subject was pursued no further. As we left them I felt that we were leaving the most wretched and hopeless of men."

Col. Gaston said that upon his return from his interview with the Youngers, inspector Reed told him the following, which has never before been made public: "A short time before the Northfield robbery," said the inspector, "I was on my way home to St. Paul from a point in Iowa. I endeavored to secure a Pullman car berth, but found that I had been preceded by two men who had engaged eight berths—the only ones remaining in the car. Later, however, I was informed that I could have one of the berths, as one of the party had failed to put in an appearance. As I sat in that car that evening a man wearing a slouch hat sat directly behind me; in the seat opposite him was a man whom I subsequently discovered was Cole Younger. While thus seated, a big, boisterous countryman, accompanied by his young lady, entered the car and demanded my seat. 'We've been to a dance and are tired'— that was his apology. I told him that his lady could sit beside me, but I didn't propose to yield my seat to a man. As we were arguing, the man in the slouch hat came over and said to me quietly, 'Why don't you throw the d—d yahoo out of the window?' I made no reply, whereupon he turned to my persecutor and said, 'Here, you d—d loafer, if you don't go about your business I'll throw you off the train. You have been dancing and enjoying yourself and I guess you can stand up awhile. This gentleman has a long way to travel, he has paid for his seat, and by G—d, he shall keep it.' This was quite enough. The big man moved off. The next day, when I was in my bank, in walked the two strange men who had secured the berths on the car. They asked for a bank almanac of last year. I told them we had none to spare; that the almanacs were issued to banks alone and were really invaluable. Then they asked if they could borrow an almanac of the previous year, and I said yes, if they would be sure to return it. As I passed it over the counter the man in the slouch hat pushed a ten dollar bill toward me. 'Take this,' said he, 'so you will be compensated if we should fail to return the book.' I reminded him he had promised to return the book—that it was part of a file and could not be spared. He insisted, however, that I should retain the money, because something might occur preventing the return of the almanac. Well, the book never came back. Three days later the Northfield Bank was robbed, and shortly afterward I identified Cole Younger as one of the two men who had taken the almanac from me. From the descriptions I have read and the pictures I have seen of the men, I am satisfied that the other man, the man with the slouched hat, the one who came to my rescue on the train, was the notorious outlaw, Jesse James."

ANECDOTES OF JESSE AND FRANK JAMES.

SOMETIMES incidents, in themselves trivial, serve to reveal the character of persons connected with them better than those actions which are esteemed as more important. The James Boys are robbers, but nevertheless they are still capable of generous actions. It may be that the remembrance of former days sometimes disposes their minds to the contemplation of the true, the beautiful and the good in humanity. Jesse James was once baptized, and became a member of a Baptist church in Clay county, Missouri, and it is said that for a considerable time before the war, his conduct was exemplary in the highest degree. But he has since sadly fallen from grace.

SOME years ago a tenant on the Samuels farm had a difficulty with the mother of Jesse and Frank. In the heat of passion he denounced the old lady as a liar. Jesse heard of the affair, and, as he always exhibited the warmest affection for his mother, those who knew of the circumstance fully expected that the tenant would be called to account in the usual way by Jesse James. One day the offending tenant was engaged in some domestic labor near his home and adjacent to a corn-field, when suddenly there was a rustling of the dry corn-blades and the next instant the dreaded outlaw leaped his horse over the fence and dashed up to the affrighted citizen with a heavy revolver ready cocked in his hand. "I have come to kill you!" he said, at the same time making an ominous motion with the pistol. "Did you not know better than to call my mother a liar? Now, if you want to make your peace with God, you had better be at it." The poor man dropped upon his knees and began to pray. As he proceeded, he became more and more fervent. He asked God to pardon his transgressions and have mercy upon him. Then he commended his loved ones to the protecting care of that Beneficent Being to whom alone they could look, now that he was so soon to be taken away from them. The prayer had become pathetic in its earnestness. As the man proceeded, the hard lines in Jesse James' features relaxed, a shade of sadness stole over his countenance, the muzzle of the pistol was unconsciously lowered, and when the poor frightened farmer had finished, the look of stern resolve was all gone, and the outlaw's pistol had been sheathed. "I cannot kill you thus," he said, "but you must leave the country," and Jesse James wheeled his horse and disappeared as he had come.

What tender reminiscences may have come to Jesse James then? Who can tell? The farmer settled up his affairs and departed from the country soon afterward. His prayer had prevailed with Jesse, and he **was spared to his loved ones.**

The following anecdote illustrates a trait prominently developed in the character of the outlaws—that is, their willingness to make personal sacrifices to serve anyone whom they regard in a friendly light.

It was during the war. Col. J. H. R. Cundiff, now editor of the St. Louis *Times*, had been in North Missouri on recruiting service for the Confederate army. The whole country was overrun by Federal soldiers, and the situation of the recruiting officers in that region was perilous. One night Col. Cundiff and several officers visited the house of Mr. Bivens, in Clay county, to obtain food and secure a trusty guide to pilot them out of that region. They learned that a man who resided some miles away was thoroughly acquainted with the by-ways of the country, and could be relied upon in such an emergency. Among all the men present not one knew the way to the house of the person whose services were sought. Miss Bivens, a beautiful and accomplished young lady, at length offered to venture through the darkness and find the guide. Frank James was there, and spoke up, "Oh, no, that is not necessary. Just get on my horse behind me, and I will take you there." The lady, who was at that time very fond of the society of the guerrilla, trusted herself with him, and mounting on the horse behind him they rode away into the night, she indicating to him the route to be taken. Though the roads were guarded by Federals, the gauntlet of pickets was successfully run, and the guide was secured. In those days Frank and Jesse James were esteemed as chivalrous gentlemen, and fit guardians of female honor. Col. Cundiff and his fellow officers were enabled to effect a change of base in comparative security, by the chivalrous services rendered by Frank James.

A story is told of Jesse, which shows that he is not impervious to the appeals of the suffering. One day he was riding in a sparsely settled region in western Texas. Passing through a belt of timber along a stream, he came to the camping place of an emigrant family. There a most distressing spectacle presented itself. The "movers" were people in indigent circumstances, evidently. The old blind horse and poor mule which had drawn the rickety wagon seemed as if their days of toil were about numbered. The man who had driven them had died there under a tree two days before; the woman was extended on the earth, almost in the agonies of death, and three children, the eldest not more than nine years of age, were crouched around, wailing piteously for something to stay the ravages of hunger.

Jesse saw the miserable condition of the unfortunate emigrant family. He at once dismounted, examined the poor sick woman, administered to her necessities as best he could, and also gave the children something to eat from his own small store of supplies. He then bid the woman be of good cheer, promised to come again before night, mounted his horse and galloped away in search of assistance. Ten miles from the camp he found a physician, and two miles further he found a coffin-maker. The first he sent to the lonely camp by the stream, the other he set to work to make a coffin. Then he found a man with a spring wagon and engaged his services. With a supply of things of present necessity, he turned once more toward the camp. Arrived there he prepared the food and made the coffee himself for the unfortunate family. The physician came and prescribed for the sick lady. The undertaker brought the coffin, and the owner of the spring wagon came to remove the bereaved woman and her little ones to a place of shelter. The stranger was buried—where?—in an untimely tomb.

> "No human hands with pious reverence rear'd,
> But the charmed eddies of autumnal winds,
> Built o'er his mouldering bones a pyramid
> Of mouldering leaves in the waste wilderness."

The bereaved one and her orphaned children were carried to the house of a pioneer some miles away, and every want was bountifully provided for, and in a pleasant farm-house she and her children call their own home, she blesses the outlaw, and prays that he may be kept from harm, and that he may be led aright at last.

THEY tell a story of Frank James which illustrates one peculiar trait of the outlaw's character—that is, his gallantry and knightly devotion to the honor of the fair sex. It happened in Kentucky. There was a young lady resident in a neighborhood where Frank James was a visitor, who had become the victim of the persecutions of a certain fellow whose addresses she had refused. On every possible occasion this low-bred person sought to mortify and insult the young lady, who was unfortunate in not having any near male relatives to champion her cause. One evening, at a social entertainment, the neighborhood coxcomb and instinctive ruffian approached the young lady in a very rude and offensive manner, just at the time when she was engaged in conversation with Frank James, who had been only a few minutes before presented to her. Without apparently noticing the insolence of the person, Frank suggested a promenade, and the young lady took his arm, and they walked away. In no long time they met the rude fellow again, and he took special pains to mortify the young lady, and threw out a gratuitous insult to her escort. Very politely Frank begged the lady to release him for a moment, and he followed the coxcomb. Coming up with him, he quietly requested him to step aside for a moment. The fellow treated the request with contempt, and added insult to injury. Without the least show of passion, Frank rejoined the lady and conducted her to her friends. He then calmly awaited his opportunity. It came that same evening. Some persons present knew the desperate character of Frank James, and had told the fellow he was in danger. The fellow attempted quietly to withdraw from the company, but he could not effect his purpose. Frank James had his attention fixed upon the ill-mannered man. When he had gone away from the house some distance, Frank arrested his progress. He had a pistol drawn, which he presented. "You deserve to die," said Frank James in a low, quiet tone, "but on one condition I will spare you, under the circumstances. Will you comply?" "Name your conditions!" responded the other, now thoroughly frightened "These:" said Frank James, "You must write a note to the lady, abjectly apologizing for your conduct. It must be done before ten o'clock to-morrow, and you must leave the country within five days, and never return. If the letter does not reach the lady by noon to-morrow, I will hunt you until I find you, and then as sure as there is a God in heaven I will kill you. If after five days you are found in this country, I will shoot you. Remember what I say!" The man promised compliance, and Frank James returned to the merry-makers, and no one who saw him suspected that the quiet gentleman had thoughts of bloodshed in his mind. The letter came, and in three days the neighborhood fop had disappeared.

BASSHAM'S CONFESSION OF THE GLENDALE ROBBERY.

THE robbery of the Chicago and Alton train at Glendale, Missouri, as already described, has been surrounded with considerable mystery, concerning the identity of all those engaged in the outrage.

The large rewards offered for the apprehension of the robber-band,—amounting to $75,000—caused a very active search, which resulted, at last, in the capture of Daniel (better known as Tucker) Bassham, under circumstances already related on page ninety-nine. The writer visited Bassham at the county jail in Kansas City, in October, 1880, for the purpose of intervieving him, with the hope of obtaining some interesting facts concerning the robbery, but though he had made a written confession, he refused to talk on the subject, saying that he had already told too much for his own good.

On the 6th day of November, Bassham was brought into court for trial, having entered a plea of "not guilty," despite his confession, but this plea was soon changed to that of "guilty," and he then threw himself upon the mercy of the court. The following summary of his confession appeared in the Kansas City *Journal* of November 7th:

"On Monday night preceding the robbery,' said Bassham in his confession, " two neighbors of mine came to me and said they had put up a job to rob a train, and wanted me to go in with them. 'I told them I didn't want nothin' to do with robbin' no train, and wouldn't have nothin' to do with it nohow; but they kept on persuadin' and finally went away, sayin' they would come back in the morning and that I must go with them. They said a very rich train was coming down on the C. & A., and that we could make a big haul, perhaps $100,000. Wa'al, that kind o' half persuaded me, but still I didn't like to go. They finally told me that Jesse James was arrangin' the thing and that it was sure to be a success.

"Wa'al, then they left. My wife kept pesterin' me to know what was goin' on an' what they wanted, but I didn't like ter let on. I kept thinking about it all night. Of course I'd heerd often of Jesse James and kinder had confidence in him, then I was pretty poor, there wasn't much crops on my place and winter comin' on, and I tell you it looked pretty nice to get a little money just then, no matter whar it kum from. 'Sides I thought to myself, ef I don't go it'll be done jest the same anyhow, they'll be down on me and ten to one I'll be more likely to git arrested if I ain't thar as if I am.

"Wa'al, I kep' kinder thinkin' it over an' in the morning they came to the house early and eat breakfast, and then went out and loafed around the timber and in the cornfield all day so nobody wouldn't see 'em. In the evenin' they all cum in and we eat supper and then they giv' me a pistol, an' we all got on our horses an' rode off together. We soon met another man on the road, an' when we got to Seaver's school-house, 'bout a mile and a half away from my house, they giv a kind of a whistle for a signal, and two men came out of the timber an' rode up. I was introduced to one of them as Jesse James. This was the first time I had ever seen Jesse James in my life."

"And who was the other?" demanded the prosecutor.

"The other was Ed. Miller, of Clay county."

Bassham said that Jesse James then gave him a shot-gun and furnished each man with a mask, and that they all then rode on in silence toward Glendale. No instructions were given to any one man. When they arrived at Glendale they noticed the light in the store, and Bassham was ordered by Jesse James to go in, capture the inmates and bring them over to the station. On looking in the windows he found the usual crowd of loiterers had left the store and lounged over to the depot to wait for the train to come in. He then went on over to the depot and found the crowd in the waiting-room guarded by one of the men. Jesse James then told him to walk up and down the platform, as the train approached, and fire off his shot-gun in the air as fast as he could. The telegraph operator was forced, at the point of the pistol, to lower the green light and thus signal the train to stop. Jesse James then asked him if there were any loose ties there that they could lay across the track, and he said he didn't know of any. The men then went and got logs and laid them across the track to obstruct the train if it should take the alarm and not stop for the green light. Meanwhile the train approached; Bassham walked up and down the platform firing off his gun; Jesse James and one of the men jumped into the express car, and Miller jumped on the engine in the manner already described and with which all are familiar. The train was not stopped more than five or six minutes.

As soon as it was over, Jesse James fired off his pistol, which was the signal for all to leave, and they jumped on their horses and rode rapidly for about half a mile, till they came to a deserted log-cabin. Here they alighted and entered. Somebody produced a small pocket-lantern and somebody else struck a match. Jesse James threw the booty down on a rude table in the middle of the compartment, divided it out, and shoved each man a pile as they stood round the table. Bassham's share was between $800 and $900. Jesse then said: "Now, each one of you fellows go home and stay there. Go to work in the morning, and keep your mouths shut, and nobody will ever be the wiser. This country will be full of men in the morning hunting for me and you."

It will be observed that in the confession, as reported, only the names of Jesse James and Ed. Miller appear, when it is now positively known that the gang comprised not less than six persons. The confession implicated two of the most respectable farmers in Jackson county, Kit Rose and Dick Tally, one a brother-in-law and the other a cousin of the Younger brothers, both of whom were arrested, but soon afterward released, as not a scintilla of evidence could be discovered corroborating Bassham's disjointed statements. The other party, who Bassham swears was connected with the robbery (and in this he certainly guessed rightly), was Jim Cummings, who shot George Shepherd in the affair at Short Creek.

In November last (1880), Bassham was brought into court with a plea of "not guilty," notwithstanding his confession, but he had so completely convicted himself that the plea was withdrawn, and he threw himself upon the mercy of the court. He was then sentenced to the penitentiary for a period of ten years. Since his confinement at Jefferson City, there has been a considerable change of opinion respecting his guilt, and there is no doubt but that now a large majority of persons believe Bassham innocent of any complicity with the train robbery, and that his so-called confession was the result of influences which the writer does not wish to assume the responsibility of naming.

The James Boys Heard From Again.

THE TRAIN ROBBÉRY AT WINSTON, MO., JULY 15, 1881.

FIFTY THOUSAND DOLLARS REWARD OFFERED FOR THE ARREST OF THE GUILTY PARTIES.

The Border Outlaws, those whose crimes began with the hot and infectious breath of war and left a bloody trail around Jackson, Clay and Harrison counties, Missouri, still survive to wreak a desperate vengeance, and live by tributes levied upon corporations and individuals. Many of the old band, it is true, have been palsied by death, dying, belted and armed, by a fate anticipated, but like the excision of a cancer, the germs have remained from which a new growth has constantly developed to harass the State and disorder society.

The James boys, aside from their reckless courage, are possessed of extraordinary capabilities, cunning resource, domineering resolution, woods-craft and dash. As if by a thorough consideration of the beneficial result to be secured thereby, they first terrorized the people of Western Missouri, and then heroized themselves in the eyes of those whose political sympathies were in consonance with their own. Thus upon the one side the people were afraid to attempt any punishment of the outlaws or give information of their rendezvous; while upon the other they were protected and encouraged without concealment. It is for these reasons that the James boys and their confreres have eluded every pursuit and been able to give free license to their impious passions.

There are peculiar features, however, connected with every outrage perpetrated by the James gang which readily manifest them in the deed. Among these several distinguishing features are: their appearance in the vicinity where the robbery occurs some days before its accomplishment; the thorough maturity of their plans; the wearing of long linen dusters; unhesitating disposition to commit murder; a splendid mount; the invariable sack carried in which to deposit the plunder; the line of retreat always southward when the robbery has been committed north of Clay county, and *vice versa;* masks of red handkerchiefs, and the ease with which pursuit is eluded. In addition to these unmistakable peculiarities, another fact is particularly noticeable, viz: within twenty-four hours after the James boys commit a robbery, Mrs. Samuels, their mother, never fails to make her appearance in Kansas City, the purpose of these visits being undoubtedly to discover what means are employed looking to the apprehension of the gang, and gather up any and all such information as might prove serviceable in aiding the escape of her sons.

Considering well all these points of evidence, any shrewd analyzer of human nature can readily determine whether or not either of the James boys was connected with any robbery reported.

On the night of July 15th, 1881, an outward going passenger train from Kansas City over the Chicago, Rock Island & Pacific Railroad was robbed at Winston Station, Daviess county, Missouri, under the following circumstances: The train left Kansas City at 6:30 P. M., in charge of William Westfall, the conductor; Wolcott, the engineer, and Charlie Murray, express messenger. The train consisted of six coaches and a sleeper, all of which were well filled with passengers. Reaching Cameron, a stop was made for supper, and when the train started off two men were observed to jump on, each of whom wore a large red bandana handkerchief around his neck, partly concealing his features. Nothing indicative of the robbers' intentions, however, transpired until the train reached Winston, at 9:30 P. M., at which station four men took passage, each having his face covered with a handkerchief identical with those worn by the two that got on at Cameron, and all wearing long linen dusters. Getting under headway again, the train had proceeded nearly one mile from Winston when suddenly, as Conductor Westfall appeared in the second car to collect tickets, the passengers were startled by the largest of the robbers rising from his seat and shouting out in a loud voice, "All aboard!" which was the signal for action. The large man, heavily masked with a red handkerchief, as were all the others, seven in number, thrust out a large pistol, and saying to Westfall, "You are the man I want," fired. The ball struck Westfall in the arm, producing only a flesh wound, but as the wounded man turned to run out of the car two more shots

DEATH OF CONDUCTOR WESTFALL.

were fired by the same robber without effect. This bad shooting seemed to exasperate another one of the outlaws, who gave an exhibition of his skill by shooting Westfall in the brain, killing him instantly, the body falling off the platform onto the ground.

While this unprovoked murder was being perpetrated three others of the outlaw gang rushed through the cars toward the engine. Wild confusion followed, and a stone mason named J. McCulloch, from Iowa, who had been working near Winston, attempted to get out of the baggage car as the robbers entered it. Suspecting that he was either the engineer or intent upon raising an alarm, one of the outlaws shot him dead and pushed his body off the train, which had now come to a stop.

The robbers then went about their business of robbing, two mounting the engine, three were left to guard the passengers, while the remaining two made for the express car. Mr. Murray, the express agent, hearing firing and suspecting the real cause, made a hasty attempt to close and lock the doors of his car, which had been left open, owing to the oppressively warm weather, but while he was thus engaged one of the robbers jumped through the partly closed door and grabbing Murray, struck him a violent blow on the head with his pistol, at the same time saying, "Open up, d—n you, or I'll kill you!" Looking into the muzzles of two large pistols, Murray was forced to comply, and delivered up the safe keys. The treasure box was quickly opened and its contents extracted, consisting of coin and currency to the amount of $8,000 or $10,000, which was thrown into a sack the outlaws carried for the purpose. The train was then started up by one of the robbers, but after proceeding a few hundred yards stopped again and the bold free-booters jumped off, running for their horses which were tied in a clump of trees less

THE SHOOTING OF J. MC CULLOCH.

than one hundred yards from the track. They did not take the time to untie their horses, but cut the reins, and mounting, rode in a half circuit around

Cameron, then took a course almost due south. They crossed the Missouri river near Sibley's Landing, in couples, having divided up immediately after the robbery was consummated.

On the morning following the robbery, an examination of the immediate vicinity about where the train was stopped, resulted in finding where the robbers had tied their horses, and there, lying on the ground, was found the following letter:

KANSAS CITY, July 12.

CHARLIE—I got your letter to-day, and was glad to hear that you had got everything ready in time for the 15th. We will be on hand at that time. Bill will be with us. We will be on the train; don't fear. We will be in the smoker at Winston. Have the horses and boys in good fix for fast work. We will make this point again on the night of the 16th. All is right here. Frank will meet us at Cameron. Look sharp and be well fixed. Have the horses well gaunted, for we may have some running to do. Don't get excited, but keep cool till right time. Wilcox or Wolcott will be on the engine. I think best to send this to Kidder. Yours time and through death.

SLICK.

After receiving the first particulars of the robbery by telegraph, I went to Kansas City, and from thence to various points in the vicinity, for the purpose of prosecuting an investigation with the view of discovering, if possible, who the outlaws were, where they came from, whither they went, and how the authorities prosecuted the pursuit. From these efforts I am prepared to state, with circumstantial positiveness, that Frank James and Jim Cummings were the parties who planned, and with the aid of their confreres, executed the robbery at Winston, and that the proof may not be wanting, the following several facts are recited:

A few weeks ago I received a letter from Frank James, acknowledging the receipt of a copy of "Border Outlaws," which I sent to him by a relative. Shortly after its receipt, this same relative, who is known to be in communication with Frank James, visited St. Louis and confidentially conferred with my publisher upon the advantages which we might mutually reap by a sudden stimulation in the sale of "Border Outlaws," for which he was then acting as agent. His proposition embraced a statement that Frank James and Jim Cummings were at that time in Missouri planning a campaign; that a large robbery would soon be consummated, attended with some startling results. All these facts he agreed to furnish us the very moment the robbery should be completed, comprising the names of those engaged, how they had organized, where assembled, cause for their acts, etc., provided my publisher would give him a certain sum of money. The incentive on our part to comply with his proposition was in securing this reliable information, which might be added as an appendix to a new edition of "Border Outlaws," and issued contemporaneously with the first newspaper reports, thereby creating a largely increased demand for the book. Of course there appeared so much doubt involved in this singular proffer, and the proposition within itself being of such questionable character, that it was rejected with little consideration of the probability of a robbery such as was declared about to take place. At this time, however, the assertions then made assume an interest which throws much light upon the problem, "Who committed the robbery?"

But this is not all the evidence I am in possession of respecting this latest adventure of the old gang. In pursuing my investigations I visited Olathe, Kas., twenty miles south of Kansas City, and there found a gentleman well known in that town, who had met Frank James walking on the south side of Olathe's public square, well-armed, on the 10th inst., or only five days before the robbery occurred. It was not a mistaken identity, for the gentleman in question was raised within four miles of the present residence of the James boys' parents, and was for years upon terms of the greatest social intimacy with them, attending the same school, participating in the same sports, and in later years meeting with them as old acquaintances. Being well acquainted myself in Olathe, I can positively state that this information regarding the presence of Frank James in the town referred to is true beyond all doubt. But what his business was or when he left, I could not ascertain.

Within eighteen hours after the robbery, Mrs. Samuels appeared in Kansas City, evidently for the purpose of collecting such information as might be useful to Frank James and his confederates. She talked freely of the robbery, but protested, with repeated declarations, that both Frank and Jesse were dead, going so far in her assertions as to say that Frank died three years ago of consumption, in Texas. What she hoped to gain by a claim so easily disproved it is difficult to conjecture.

From the best evidence attainable, the gang who robbed the Rock Island and Pacific train, among whom were Frank James, Ed. Miller, Jim Cummings and Dick Little, after leaving the train, mounted their horses and rode southwestwardly until they reached the outskirts of Cameron, when they turned and took to the brush again, making directly for the Missouri river, which they crossed near Sibley's landing, and on the following evening, the 16th, they certainly passed through Sni-a-bar township of Jackson county, and, taking a southwestwardly course, continued on to the Indian Territory. The party, however, did not remain intact, but divided up into couples, so as to destroy the trail which so large a number as seven riders would have made conspicuous. They were at no time so far apart, though, but that a prearranged signal would have concentrated the outlaws.

It is a singular fact that with all the atrocious crimes credited to the James boys and their confederates, there was not so much as one dollar of reward offered at the time of the Winston robbery, although at one time the rewards offered by the State and railroad and express companies aggregated $75,000. During Gov. Hardin's administration nearly all the rewards offered by the State were withdrawn, then the private corporations that had suffered so seriously at the hands of the bold knights of the road withdrew the incentives they had advertised, after which Gov. Phelps wiped out the few figures remaining.

On the 26th of July, eleven days after the train robbery at Winston, Governor Crittenden visited St. Louis and called a meeting of leading railroad officials in the gentlemen's parlor of the Southern Hotel. The call was responded to by representatives from nearly all the principal roads running into Kansas City and St. Louis, and upon assembling plans were thoroughly discussed for the apprehension of the notorious outlaws who have wrought such injury to Missouri's reputation. The session lasted for nearly four hours, though there was the greatest unanimity of feeling and disposition, and at its conclusion the Governor expressed much gratification at the results. The power of the Executive is limited by law, so that he could not offer a State reward sufficiently large to accomplish the arrest of such notorious desperadoes as the James boys and their gang are known to be, so he conceived the excellent idea of calling upon the interested railroad corporations for needful assistance. The result of this conference was the immediate issuance of a proclamation by Governor Crittenden, in which an aggregate reward of fifty-five thousand dollars ($55,000) was offered for the capture of the seven train robbers, or five thousand dollars for the arrest and conviction of each one of the robber gang. This proclamation was supplemented by the offer of an additional reward of five thousand dollars each for the arrest of Jesse and Frank James, and delivery of their bodies to the sheriff of Daviess County, and a further reward of five thousand dollars each for their conviction.

The public which, generally speaking, believe that Jesse James was never shot by Geo. Shepherd, credit the assertion made by many that both Frank and Jesse were engaged in the Winston robbery, but whatever the impression, this belief is undoubtedly without foundation. The most intimate acquaintances of Jesse James, those who have seen him many times during the past year, are ready to make oath that he is a paralytic from the effects of Geo. Shepherd's shot; in fact, in a demented, helpless condition.

At one time arrangements were about perfected, through the outlaws' cousin, by which I was to have a personal interview with Frank James, each of us to be accompanied by a friend, but owing to some engagement, which was never explained to me, that meeting never occurred. Frank, after receiving a copy of "Border Outlaws," expressed a desire to make a statement, with the understanding that I would embody it in all subsequent editions of the book; this I agreed to do, but I am now convinced that the intended interview was not granted because of the engagement which was kept at Winston.

www.ingramcontent.com/pod-product-compliance
Lightning Source LLC
Chambersburg PA
CBHW020307170426
43202CB00008B/531